Urbanization in Developing Countries

The 'young towns' of Lima: aspects of urbanization in Peru

Urbanization in Developing Countries

edited by Kenneth Little

The 'young towns' of Lima

Aspects of urbanization in Peru

PETER LLOYD
Professor of Social Anthropology
University of Sussex

CAMBRIDGE UNIVERSITY PRESS

Cambridge
London   New York   New Rochelle
Melbourne   Sydney

Published by the Press Syndicate of the University of Cambridge
The Pitt Building, Trumpington Street, Cambridge CB2 1RP
32 East 57th Street, New York, NY 10022, USA
296 Beaconsfield Parade, Middle Park, Melbourne 3206, Australia

First published 1980

Phototypeset in V.I.P. Times by
Western Printing Services Ltd. Bristol
Printed in Great Britain at the University Press, Cambridge.

British Library Cataloguing in Publication Data
Lloyd, Peter Cutt
The 'young towns' of Lima. – (Urbanization in
developing countries).
1. Squatter settlements – Peru – Lima – Case
studies   2. Medalla Milagrosa, Lima – Social
conditions   3. Lima – Social conditions
I. Title   II. Series
309.1′85′2   HD7329.L5   79–41644
ISBN 0 521 22871 9 hard covers
ISBN 0 521 29688 9 paperback

Contents

Maps

Preface

The mass migration of peasants to the cities is a recent phenomenon common to most nations of the Third World. As traditional modes of agriculture stagnate, and policies of land reform or mechanization rarely provide many opportunities, the movement to the cities, with their growing manufacturing industry, and their increased public bureaucracies, is seen to be the only way of achieving a more modern way of life. Recurrent themes in the study of this migration are the psychological adaptation of the peasant to the bustle and competitiveness of city life, the paucity of wage employment compared with the migrant flow, and the consequent development of the informal sector of self-employed artisans, petty traders and the like. Planners try in vain to cope with an urban growth in which perhaps half of the city population lives not merely in poverty, but in grossly substandard housing. The new slums are seen by the affluent as belts of misery, cancerous sores, sources of disease and violence. This popular image contrasts, however, with studies which stress the role of kinship networks in helping the migrants adjust to city life, the essentially conservative attitude of many of the slum residents, their determination to build their own homes and to educate their children, so that they may avail themselves of opportunities lost to their parents.

Each nation experiences the same process, however much local culture and ecology serve to accentuate the visible contrasts. One may generalize, as I have done in *Slums of Hope?* (1979), and provide analyses and explanations which seem valid across many countries. Descriptions of individual countries tend, if they focus one the more basic phenomena of the urbanization process, to display a substantial similarity. Hence I have tried in this book to present a more idiosyncratic approach, focusing upon a single community in Lima, Peru's capital, and seeing in its own development an example of the wider social process.

In part, this approach is the consequence of the manner in which I carried out my research. I spent six months in Lima, July–December 1975, with the aim of experiencing life in a South American state; I had planned, too, to study one small slum area, thinking perhaps that I might be able to join an ongoing research project in one of the large peripheral squatter settlements. Instead I discovered Medalla Milagrosa – a clearly bounded community of some hundred households – only two blocks from my house, the anthropologist's gift. I thus divided my time between the study of the small settlement and the attempt to gain an overview of the urbanization process through documentary material and perambulations across the city.

Much has been written on Lima, about its squatter settlements and slums, and about its poor, though relatively little of this is the result of academic research. Little has been written about specific communities; social anthropologists tend to follow up in the urban area the migrants from their previously studied village; but as these migrants are dispersed throughout the city, the focus of study is therefore their relationship with their migrant co-villagers. For some, the anthropological study of the small community is a retrograde step because the community is not seen as part of the wider urban environment, nor as the consequence of government policies, or of economic processes. Furthermore, each urban neighbourhood is so clearly different from its neighbours that one cannot, as in the classic anthropological monographs, presume that one's own village is typical of the entire tribe.

The urban anthropologist is conscious of the need to see his own little community in the wider social context, to see its formation both as a consequence of ongoing processes and as contributing to those processes. But the study of such a dialectical process is not easy. One is trying to get a 'worm's-eye view' and a 'bird's-eye view' almost simultaneously; at one moment one is completely immersed in the life of the little community, at the next far distant from it. From an actor-oriented approach as one watches the individual coping with his everyday problems of living, one jumps to a structural approach in which the individual becomes a mere cipher.

Again, the urban anthropologist, who usually studies slums rather than affluent areas, becomes involved in the welfare of his subjects. He is not merely interested in change, but is anxious to promote change. In the urban area the impact of state agencies in their great variety is much greater than is usual in the countryside. Typically the anthropologist assumes a dual role. He reports the impact of policies on the recipient community, often having to indicate their negligible effect on many, their deleterious effect on a few. He may indeed suggest improvements, though unless he is a member of the planning agency, his words are likely to carry little weight; the plans move forward inexorably. Alternatively, he may articulate the demands of his community, describing how its people see their world, and what they want from it; here too the anthropologist experiences personal frustration. But in both he tends to take as given the economic processes of the city, and the government policies and plans, studying instead their impact on the recipient or the recipients' reactions. What is needed is the anthropological study of both planners and recipients, of the way in which each group perceives the world in general and the other in particular, the manner in which the

policies of the former and the reactions of the latter are consequent upon
their respective perceptions. In other words we seek a genuinely dialectical approach.

This, however, is both difficult to present and, in the given urban
situation, difficult for an individual scholar to achieve. Perhaps the
answer lies in a team, not of members specializing in different branches of
the social sciences as so often advocated, but of social anthropologists
working at different levels of social activity – some in the community,
others in planning agencies, municipal offices and the like – and meeting
regularly to compare findings.

This is an ideal not realized in this book but derived from thoughts
about how I might have written it had I had far more time in the field, and
far more colleagues and assistants to work on different aspects of the
study. However, I have tried to set my description of one little community
within the wider framework of Lima's urban development.

My research in Lima – a preliminary visit in 1973, a stay of six months in
1975 and a brief return visit in August 1977 – was financed variously by
the Social Science Research Council and the University of Sussex whose
generosity is here acknowledged. In Lima I owe the success of my work in
Medalla Milagrosa to my two assistants, Cristina Herencia, a lecturer in
Social Psychology at the Universidad Nacional Mayor de San Marcos, and
Sonia Becerra, a final-year student in Social Anthropology at the Pontificia Universidad Católica, and to Juana Pinzas and Manuel Ortíz who
worked for shorter periods. The Faculty at both these universities
provided stimulating advice and comment, and friendship, especially Luis
Millones, Teófilo Altamirano and Jorge Osterling. The people of
Medalla Milagrosa were at first highly suspicious of the attentions of yet
more investigation from outside, wasting their time and bringing no
apparent benefit; but within a few weeks a relationship was established,
the warmth of which surpassed all our expectations.

Medalla Milagrosa is not a pseudonym; it would have been impossible
to conceal the identity of the community and its leaders without a gross
distortion of the ethnographic material. In reporting this I have omitted
much that might damage or give offence to those concerned; I trust that
the *pobladores* (settlers) will accept that this version of their lives and
problems is presented with the greatest sympathy and respect.

To them this book is dedicated in gratitude.   P.L.

Note: All monetary figures are expressed in terms of the Peruvian currency, the *sol*. In the mid-1960s £1 was the approximate equivalent of
S/.75; in the first half of the 1970s S/.100 approximated to £1. Figures
have not been corrected for inflation.

1. Introduction: the problems defined

Lima is one of the oldest of the colonial cities of Latin America, founded by Francisco Pizarro in January 1535, only two years after his defeat of the Inca king, Atahualpa, and the subsequent entry into his imperial capital, Cuzco. Originally named Ciudad de los Reyes – City of the Kings – Lima lies on the banks of the Rimac river about 11 kilometres from its mouth, where a small fishing village was to develop into Callao, Peru's principal port and now, in effect, a suburb of the metropolis. The city lay close to the foothills of the Andes, the arid mountainsides providing a panoramic background. The fertile valley had long been settled and the famed temple of Pachacamac, a few kilometres to the south of Lima, had for a millennium been an important centre of pilgrimage. Though well within the tropics, this Peruvian coast enjoys a mild, equable climate; for nine months of the year low cloud and mists keep the daily temperatures between 10° C and about 16° C. This was preferable, for most of the colonists, to the difficulties of life at high altitudes, though a few did expressly prefer the clear mountain skies. The risk of earthquakes was greater in Lima than in the sierra, though cities in the latter have suffered. Most significant, however, was the fact that while the Inca capital of Cuzco was in the heart of the Andes at a height of 2,400 metres, Lima looked outwards to the western world, and specifically towards Spain.

Lima developed quickly to become the capital of a viceroyalty which embraced areas, now not only within Peru, but also in neighbouring Ecuador, Bolivia and Chile. Its premier university, that of San Marcos, is the oldest in the continent. At the beginning of the seventeenth century the population of Lima was 25,000; half of this total comprised negroes and mulattoes, for slaves were imported by the colonists for domestic duties, the indigenous Indian being deemed too uncouth for this type of work. Almost two centuries later this population had doubled, but although Lima remained the largest city, it was closely followed by the major provincial centres: Arequipa (36,000), Cuzco (25,000) and Trujillo (12,000) (Dobyns and Doughty 1976, p. 124).

Much of the colonial city of Lima is still preserved. Narrow streets overhung by the ornate wooden balconies of the wealthier residences divide the area into regular blocks 120 metres square. Many huge and highly ornate baroque churches have served the city's population. These remain; so too do many of the homes of the aristocracy, though whilst a

1

few are preserved – the Torre Tagle Palace, for instance, is now the headquarters of the foreign ministry – many others are falling into decay. The colonial city is now Lima's main shopping and business centre; old buildings, weakened by earthquakes, are being torn down to be replaced by modern office blocks. Some of the streets are being widened, while others are choked with street-vendors and vehicular traffic. The exhaust fumes from the latter are trapped under the low cloud to give Lima one of the most toxic atmospheres in the world.

During the colonial period Lima grew, even though slowly. The satellite settlement of Rimac developed across the river, as did the port of Callao. In both these places, too, the older buildings succumbed to inner-city decay. At the end of the nineteenth century the city expanded east and south with the creation of the suburbs of Barrios Altos and La Victoria for the poorer sections of the population. The rich developed the beach communities of Magdalena, Miraflores and Barranco, where their modest summer homes were still separated from the capital by several kilometres of farmland.

Lima's rapid growth is a phenomenon of the mid-twentieth century. At the beginning of this century its population (including that of Callao) numbered only 150,000. This figure had grown to a third of a million by 1930, to half a million in 1940, $1\frac{1}{2}$ million in 1961, and $3\frac{1}{2}$ million in 1975. This growth can be expressed as a consequence of the massive emigration from the provincial towns and countryside of youths seeking more profitable employment, and of the increase in jobs in the city with the expansion of public services and industrialization. The transformation of the heart of the colonial city into the capital's commercial centre has already been cited. Peripheral areas have been cleared to make way for new highways, ring roads and impressive modern building developments; that of the new civic centre and Sheraton Hotel being the most outstanding. Industrial areas have been developed principally along the roads linking Lima and Callao, and leading eastward from Lima into the sierra. This process of change and development has led to decay in the inner-city areas, which now provide only slum accommodation for the downwardly mobile and, on a much larger scale, for the waves of migrants. The grand mansions are let to innumerable families; these and tenement blocks fall into disrepair as rent controls inhibit renovation by landlords without doing much to ease the burden on the poor.

The richer residents moved out of the city to develop their own affluent suburbs along the roads to the beach resorts. Before the 1960s this development usually took the form of individual initiative. Since then large property companies have constructed vast estates which are not only filling in the few remaining areas between the main radial arteries of the city, but extending beyond to Monterrico, the new fashionable suburb whose slight elevation and distance from the coast gives it a little more sun that the rest of the city. But almost nothing was done, either by the state, by large private companies or by small landlords, to provide housing for the poor. Until the 1930s alleys of small single- or double-room habitations – *callejones* – were built to house the city poor. But as the inner-city slums became increasingly over-crowded, and as fresh and peripheral areas decayed to provide cheaper accommodation, so too did urban renewal and profitable forms of development deplete the quantity of housing available to the poor. Vacant lots in residential areas – the *corralones* – were filled by enterprising occupants with squalid shacks, rented to migrants. The most striking response of the poor has, however, been the invasion of land and the building of their own homes without outside assistance. Thus have the *barriadas* (squatter settlements), or *pueblos jóvenes* (young towns) as they are now designated, been created. At first areas close to the city were seized: areas which were deemed unfit for better housing, such as the steep slopes of the hills or the river banks. Later, locations usually much larger in extent were invaded: undulating and sandy land stretching for several kilometres along the roads leading north and south from the city.

Thus we see in Lima a number of distinct zones: first, an inner-city area in which decayed slums are juxtaposed with modern commercial edifices; second, peripheral to this, we find an intermediate area of modest and mixed housing; finally, on the outskirts, and growing at a phenomenal rate, are two markedly contrasting forms of urban development – on one hand, the estates built by the large private developers, and on the other, the squatter settlements constructed by the residents themselves. The houses in the former tend to be available only to the wealthiest 15 per cent of the city's population; in the latter now live half of the city's poor – the other half being in the inner-city slums and corralones. It is with these squatter settlements that this book is concerned.

The process of urban growth, chronicled here for Lima, is in no way unusual. Other large Peruvian towns have developed in a similar way, and they too have their pueblos jóvenes created by invasions in the same manner as those of Lima. Thus 37 per cent of the population of Arequipa is now located in these settlements and 64 per cent of that in Trujillo. Cuzco in contrast has very few pueblos jóvenes (21 per cent), for though it remains an important administrative and market centre, it has attracted little manufacturing industry (ONEC 1973). On the other hand, in Chimbote, a new fishing and industrial town, almost all of its people live in pueblos jóvenes. However, one does not see in these towns the same development of estates for the rich. The centralization of government and business in Lima has drawn the middle classes to the capital; regional devolution is frequently discussed but with little or no consequence.

A striking feature of the example of Lima is the manner in which the city has grown so much faster than other urban centres. At the end of the eighteenth century, Arequipa, Peru's second city, was two-thirds the size of Lima (and in fact had a larger 'Spanish colonist' population). Today Lima is fifteen times the size of its nearest rival. The capital contains almost a quarter of the country's population, compared with only 5 per cent at the earlier period. The increasing primacy of the national capital, especially where it is also a port, is a feature common to most developing countries; it is merely the exaggerated degree of primacy which makes Lima outstanding. A number of factors appear responsible for this. Most of Peru's wealth has come from its mines, and as these have been located in the high mountains, they have not given rise to large urban centres. Most of the capitals of the country's departments and constituent provinces have been very small towns of 10–20,000 people, little more than local market centres in fact, and these have provided no incentive for industrial development. Communications within Peru remain poor; most of the roads linking the sierra towns are still untarred and no railway system unites the country. The larger provincial towns recruit migrants, largely unskilled, from their hinterland whilst exporting their own sons, better educated than average, to the capital. Thus the pueblos jóvenes of Arequipa are peopled by villagers from neighbouring Cuzco and Puno departments, whilst the wealthy residents of Lima include a high proportion of Arequipans, proud of their origins; the headquarters of the Arequipa Club in Lima is certainly the grandest of all the provincial club centres.

Lima is in no way unique in housing such a large proportion of its population in squatter settlements or shanty towns. Equally striking figures obtain in the cities of developing countries in each of the continents. Lima is, however, interesting for the dramatic manner in which large areas of land have been invaded and for the manner in which the invaders are trying, with varying degrees of government toleration and encouragement, to develop the settlements into decent, if poor, residential suburbs.

The overwhelming primacy of Lima would seem to be largely a geographical accident, a result of the nature of the country's wealth, its topography and the boundaries drawn by colonial powers. But other cities, Dakar in Senegal for example, are similarly dominant. Nor does the rate of urban growth – in terms of the proportion of the population in urban centres – seem in Peru to be dissimilar to that of other South American countries, given their individual wealth and historical development. But rates of urbanization in this continent are higher than those currently found in most of Africa or Asia, because of the much later development of manufacturing industry in these continents and the relative absence of marked changes in patterns of rural landholding.

It is fortuitous that my own fieldwork experience has embraced two contrasting patterns of urban development: those of Lima and of Lagos in Nigeria. In many African cities, Nairobi for example, whose squatter settlements were described by Ross (1973) and by Hake (1977), the migrant poor have been forced, through lack of any viable alternative, to seize land and build their own homes. But in much of West Africa a different pattern evolved. In the absence of a large settled white or Asian community, who monopolized the spheres of petty commerce and artisanal activities, the early migrants were able to attain positions of relative affluence. They were able to purchase small plots of land from the indigenous communities; here the peripheral areas of cities were not owned by the state, by expatriate companies or by landed oligarchy. On these plots they built homes for themselves of such a size and style that they could let rooms to other migrants, often keeping the top floor for themselves and setting aside the ground floor for tenants. Sharing a house in this way posed no cultural difficulties, for landlord and tenant shared similar rural origins. Overcrowding and high rents certainly existed, and still do exist, but the migrants themselves have been able to provide accommodation for almost all the poor who have, in recent years, moved to the cities. Subsidiary factors support this process. Migrants *en masse* are less likely to invade land held by local lineages, while for single migrants, the effectiveness of actions for eviction in the customary courts makes illegal seizure impracticable. Again, many migrants prefer to build their own houses in their rural home areas (against an anticipated return) and thus have less interest in building in the city.

The situation in Lima is in direct contrast to this. The dominant white and *mestizo* groups have done almost nothing to provide housing for the poor sierra Indian migrant, and sharing accommodation (save in the domestic servant relationship) is out of the question. These dominant groups block the migrant's rise to affluence; he cannot afford a house on even the cheapest estates, and there is virtually no means of legally acquiring a small plot of land on which to build, for the periphery of Lima is composed of the *haciendas* (estates) of the landed oligarchy. The migrant who has settled in the inner-city area in order to establish himself may either choose to build his own home in preference to paying rent or be forced out by slum clearance. In either case, invasion or residence in an existing squatter settlement seems the only viable alternative. Mass invasions increased in scale and frequency because they were clearly tolerated by the government which saw in such events a relatively cheap way of easing the housing problem. Invasion was feasible because much of the land so seized has been flat or undulating and thus easy to plan (overnight, the invaders mark out all the streets and individual plots in a regular fashion). Invasion is also feasible because of Lima's climate. The damp chilly air can be unpleasant and unhealthy but rain does not fall and a family *can* live for months in a matting hut pending the accumulation of such savings as enable them to build with mud, brick or concrete blocks.

A recent book (Guerrero de los Ríos and Sánchez León 1977) graphically contrasts the housing estates of the rich and the squatter settlements of the poor. In the former, the infrastructural services – roads, water, light – are provided, the houses are built, and then the people move in; in the latter the people move in, and *then* struggle to build their homes and obtain rudimentary services.

As noted already, the peripheral areas of Lima are now being developed by huge companies in which the interests of local landowners, construction firms and loan agencies, both Peruvian and foreign, are variously combined. Ususally the company builds all the houses in a small range of styles. Some schemes do exist, of course, for owners to build homes to their own specifications. The houses are purchased through mortgage arrangements of a conventional nature. However, the cost of these houses, the size of the down-payment required, and the security guaranteed by a regular income, make them unavailable to over three-quarters of the city's population.

In the squatter settlement the invaders first lay out the site and erect their matting huts; they then try to obtain security of tenure either *de facto* in the apparent acquiescence of the government or *de jure* through legal recognition and the grant of a title. Legal recognition is often said to be a prerequisite for building, but the settlers of Lima appear to feel that, though illegal in that it may not conform to building regulations, a decent house is one form of protection against subsequent eviction. The settlers seek the installation of piped water and electricity, the provision of sewerage, tarred roads, a local school for their children and similar amenities. A feature of the pueblos jóvenes of Lima is that their residents have been comparatively successful in the sense that, as data below show, many settlements have obtained these services, though many more still lack them.

The pueblos jóvenes are not settlements of the apathetic poor; they are vibrant with activity. Much of this activity is confined within the family. People build their own homes with little assistance, save some technical help from friends and neighbours. They are continually engaged in improving their jobs, exploiting new opportunities. They struggle to pay for their children's education. Much of their activity is, however, of a collective nature. Migrants resident in the inner city plan the invasion, and the invaders must appear as a united group both in resisting any attempts to evict them, and in obtaining legal recognition. The installation of services depends heavily on the ability of the squatters to provide communal labour and a financial contribution, for it is generally held that a settlement should pay in full for any benefits gained.

Thus the structure of these settlements should be a prime focus of our interest. What relationships continue to bind the residents after the initial invasions? To what extent do these relationships promote or impede activity, either individual or collective, in developing these settlements or in improving the lives of the individual residents? Greater poignancy is added to this last question in that the Peruvian government, in the past decade, has pursued policies in which the pueblo joven is seen as a unit through the issue of legal title to land and the installation of services, is the prime means by which poverty is ameliorated.

The social relationships of the urban poor may be studied within three arenas: those of work, residential community (that is, people who live in a given area) and ethnic group.

For the economists it is the first of these three which is of prime concern. Most of their work tends to deal with the poor in general; the nature of the formal and informal sectors of the economy and the linkages between them, the effects of wage rates on migration and a host of like issues. Studies of individual factories are very rare, and I know of no such studies in a Peruvian town, though Julian Laite's work (1977) on the copper refinery at La Oroya, which focuses upon migrant workers from two rural communities, might be said to fall into this category. Studies of individual occupational groups within the city are equally rare, though in Lima, as in many other cities, some attention has been given to street-traders, for these are seen as a problem by municipal authorities. The results of Alison Scott's study of artisans in the informal sector, showing their career patterns, remain unpublished (but see MacEwen Scott 1978).

Social anthropologists have tended to focus upon the ethnic group. Most of them carry out their initial fieldwork in a small village and then, when they find themselves for one reason or another in the city, their first inclination is to trace the migrants from this village. Their attention is thus drawn towards the urban relationships, both formal and informal, among migrants from the single community, and towards the ties maintained individually and collectively by these migrants with the home community. They also focus on the persistence of rural attitudes and traits, and the role of the ethnic group in helping the new migrant to adapt to town life. This pattern is certainly apparent in anthropological work in Peru. William Mangin, one of the first to study squatter settlements, worked originally in the Cornell University project in the village of Vicos. He and his colleague Paul Doughty 'discovered' the village clubs in the barriadas and described them in terms very familiar to students of African urban voluntary associations (Mangin 1959; Doughty 1970, 1972). Such clubs had not previously attracted attention and may well be a phenomenon peculiar, in Latin America, to Peru. Roberts (1974) has contrasted the continuing attachment of the sierra Indian of Peru to his natal community with the absence of such ties among the *ladinos* (mestizos) of Guatemala. In fact, within Peru it seems likely that clubs are much more strongly developed in respect of Indian rural communities than of mestizo ones.

Jongkind (1974) has stressed the difference between the village clubs which help the migrant to assimilate into urban life and the clubs representing departments and provinces which are for the wealthy and educated, membership of which is achieved after years of successful urban residence. In the African context it has been the practice to contrast the development of such voluntary associations in different ethnic groups in the city. Scholars in Peru have gone beyond this to discuss differences in club organization and membership within the same general culture. Thus Skeldon (1976) has postulated a historical progression and development as migrants are absorbed into urban life and lose touch with their rural community of origin. Altamirano (1977) has described the differences in function between the club of a remote rural village and that of a small but prosperous commercial centre in the Mantaro valley. The work of Long (1973) on Mantaro valley entrepreneurs and of Alderson-Smith (1975) indicates the way in which individual men either take part in or excuse themselves from full participation in club activities according to their current economic needs; for some the relationships made in the club are essential to their prosperity, for others they constitute an encumbrance. The emphasis given by social anthropologists to 'urban ethnicity' (a concept describing ties between migrants from the same rural area) contributes to a justifiable accusation that they have ignored so many of the other intracity relationships established by the migrant. (The situation is reversed in Britain where the 'problems' created by ethnic minorities are so much to the fore that a book such as Watson's (1977) which emphasizes the ties remaining with the natal communities is seen as supplying a neglected aspect of the picture.) In comparison with the vast quantity of literature on urban ethnicity, that focusing upon the residential community is slight, both in Peru and elsewhere.

Questionnaire surveys do of course tend to be based upon the territorial unit (this is a unit of analysis defined by area or territory). In Lima and other Peruvian cities a vast amount of material, most of it of very indifferent quality, has been collected by students, social workers and the like as part of class projects. Many undergraduate theses written by university students begin with a theoretical debate on the nature of marginality, continue with a history of the settlement and conclude with statistics of family size and composition, occupation and place of origin of the residents. (Medalla Milagrosa, to be described below, was the subject of one such thesis by a graduate in social work from the University of San Marcos – Nieto 1974.) Such surveys do not examine the structure of relationships within the unit.

The works of Peattie (1968) on Venezuela, Safa (1974) on Puerto Rico, Roberts (1973) on Guatemala, and Lomnitz (1977) on Mexico are prominent among the few examples of community-based studies in Latin America. For Peru no such published studies exist as yet. Lobo's (1977) thesis on a pueblo joven near Callao concentrates upon the patterns of family relationships existing within the community; its value is enhanced by the fact that she lived in the settlement at three periods within a ten-year span. Uzzell's (1972) thesis contrasts the character and personality of four pueblos jóvenes in Lima, and in so doing he emphasizes the statistical differences between them rather than the degree to which each might be said to constitute a community.

Several reasons might be adduced to explain the social anthropologist's reluctance to study the urban residential community, when holistic community studies have been one of the basic tenets of his discipline. First is the tendency already noted to study the migrants from the village already known to one. Second, while one rural village looks much like its neighbour, the urban territorial unit one chooses is so obviously unlike others: it may be more or less progressive, apathetic, developed and so on. It is clearly atypical and one seeks others for comparison, and inevitably spends less time in each, growing more dependent upon statistical data than upon participant observation. Third, it is a matter for empirical investigation to ascertain how far the territorial units do have such a pattern of internal relationships that would justify terming them communities. If formed by slow aggregation their residents may well have as few ties with their neighbours as one generally associates with a middle-class suburban street. Yet in Peru the relationships implied in the initial invasion and the existence of settlement councils suggest some degree of cohesion, though it may well be a statistical accident that the settlements studied by both Lobo and myself (and that studied by Lomnitz in Mexico City) contain a substantial proportion of residents coming from a single village. Lastly, no study of an urban squatter settlement can be oblivious to the poverty of the residents; yet this poverty cannot be explained by processes internal to the settlement. The social anthropologist who does study the residential community may find himself attacked for failing to describe the relationship of this community to the wider world. Those who studied remote and primitive communities in the 1930s could justify their presentation of them as isolates; the contemporary urban anthropologist cannot abstract his little community from the city of which it forms a constituent part. A fear of failure to do so may drive him to pose different problems.

I would argue, however, that it is imperative that the social anthropologist studies the residential community. As is well known, a few wage
earners in the formal sector of the economy belong to active and well-
organized trade unions; the greater number, being casually employed,
are not so strongly unionized and few ties exist between co-workers.
Similarly, self-employed traders and artisans lack collective organizations,
except perhaps where they share an ethnic identity. Again the ethnic ties
linking migrants are, for many of them, undoubtedly strong and their
importance cannot be minimized. But much of one's daily life is enacted
within the residential community; ties of kinship, marriage and friendship
unite neighbours in varying degrees. Attitudes are likely to derive as
much from experiences within the residential community as from the
work-place or natal village. For a man who belongs to no trade union or
village club, the community may be the only formal association of which
he is a member. Furthermore, in Peru as in some other Latin American
states, almost his only link with government and its agencies is through
membership of the community. The community thus plays a vital role
both in conditioning his perception of the world about him and in providing the arena in which he may do something to change that world to his
own advantage.

When one studies the small residential community one may well find,
as I did in Medalla Milagrosa, that it has many of the characteristics of a
little village. The people have a strong sense of corporate identity and
residents are bound together in an innumerable number of cross-cutting
interpersonal relationships. It becomes so easy and tempting to treat the
settlement as an isolate, in the same way as many anthropologists have
written as if the only relationships of the urban migrant were with co-
members of his village of origin. We *must* establish the relationship
between the settlement and its residents and the wider urban society. On
the one hand we may study the formal relationships between the settlement and urban government; on the other hand we may test the usefulness of concepts used in defining the urban poor by applying them to the
individual residents of the settlement. These tasks I undertake in later
chapters.

In Latin America the debate about urban poverty in the last two
decades has been centred upon the concept of marginality. This concept
of marginality seems to be derived from that of the 'marginal man', a
concept popular in American sociology in the 1950s which describes a
person crossing a social barrier, perhaps one of ethnicity or class. Variously the marginal or incompletely integrated man was described as being
either apathetic or exceptionally creative and innovative. In its former
sense the term seemed applicable in the Latin American urban situation:
the rural emigrant was slow to integrate into urban life.

Writers of many theoretical persuasions have found the term useful, and its connotations now range very widely. 'The marginals' has tended to become a popular euphemism for the poor; it is a highly ambiguous term, for it is often unclear whether all the poor are embraced – that is, well over half the urban population including all residents of inner-city slums and squatter settlements – or whether it is only the bottom 10 per cent of the population to which reference is being made. Again one not only has marginal people but marginal settlements: those on land deemed unsuitable for building; marginal houses: those not in accord with building rules; marginal occupations: those which generally yield low and irregular incomes. But a man working in a marginal occupation may have a relatively good income and he may have built himself a decent house though in a settlement deemed marginal.

The usages of the term may be reduced to two broad categories: marginality in the sense of 'not integrated into', and 'excluded from'. The former usually implies a dualist view of society: people are moving from one sector of society to another but have yet to be fully incorporated into the other. The latter implies a monist view: people are driven away from, or prevented from participating in, the dominant culture and its institutions.

In Peru the term *cholo* designated the migrant with predominantly Indian cultural origins who, in the city, adopted western dress, the Spanish language and similar traits; he was unlike the mestizo, who emphasized his full attachment to Spanish culture by his continuing close links with his rural community and apparent adherence to its values. For the middle classes of Lima the term 'cholo' was usually one of abuse, a reference to the poor migrant who seemed to be too assertive of his urban status. For most such people in the dominant sector of Peruvian city society saw the massive immigration as a threat to their cherished way of life. The term 'cholofication' used by academic writers reflected a deep fear among the wealthier classes of Lima. Quijano, a leading Peruvian sociologist now prominent in radical circles, exemplified the conjunction of popular attitudes and scholarly theses. In his doctoral thesis (1965) he described the emergence of the cholo and assessed the significance of this group for Peruvian society. He saw the cholo in three dimensions: sociological – the lack of a clear pattern of norms; cultural – the ambivalence between Spanish and Indian cultures; and psychological – a conflict in personality patterns. Quijano saw in the cholo a new element in Peruvian society, one which would not be completely assimilated into the dominant culture. Among its consequences would be the impetus given to nationalistic ideologies, a greater integration of Indian and *criollo* (coastal) cultures and an increased communication between the Indian and the rest of the society, as the cholo, in his rural home, would become an innovator and a leader of radical movements.

In many ways the cholo parallels the 'detribalized African' discussed in so much of the literature of that continent in the 1950s. The mode of definition leads one to focus upon the processes of adjustment where an individual is seemingly torn from his own culture and can only slowly integrate himself into the new urban culture. Psychological studies carried out in Lima tended to confirm the traumatic consequences of migration. The migrant from the sierra village was seen as suffering not only culture shock but extreme physical discomfort in moving from very high altitudes to sea level. Seguin found, in his psychiatric clinic, migrants who had no major physical explanation of sickness but who suffered anxiety and depression, which he saw as psychosomatically produced by a nostalgia for their home areas and which aggravated physical symptoms. Fried (1959), an American doctor working in the barriada of San Cosme in association with Seguin, found a population disillusioned with life in Lima, lacking contacts with other migrants and, in their isolation, retreating into Indian cultural habits: the chewing of coca and the drinking of *chicha* beer. Such themes recur in later studies but the statistical evidence produced, whilst demonstrating less urban adjustment among recent migrants and more sickness among the poor, does not show that sickness is necessarily the product of depression.

The view of an apathetic migrant population was popular among the wealthier people for it both sustained their fears of the poor and explained the causes of their poverty. This image was dispelled by Mangin (1960) who lived in the barriada of Comas, founded in the late 1950s, and who, more than any other anthropologist writing of urban Latin America in the 1960s, emphasized the vitality and drive for achievement in the squatter settlement. He argued strongly that residents here did not display a 'culture of poverty', as defined by Oscar Lewis, for many of the traits associated with that culture were national ones; again many psychological traits seen in the Indian migrant to the city and attributed to maladjustment were in fact common in the rural areas. The thesis that the migrant is slow to integrate has been attacked on many fronts: for instance, Mangin stressing the adherence to the dominant cultural values and Portes (1972) (writing specifically of Chile) emphasizing the rationality of the slum-dweller. Arguments that the poor are not politically integrated have been challenged by those who question the definition of participation, showing that the migrant or squatter settlement resident is as likely as others to vote, and to belong to political parties and trade unions. Perlman (1976) has summed up these approaches in her study of Brazilian *favelas*, claiming that the quality which characterizes the residents of these settlements is not marginality but poverty. The 'myth of marginality' sustains conventional middle-class attitudes towards the poor.

In the economic sphere the concept of marginality, meaning non-integrated, plays a similar role. No observer can fail to contrast the estates of modern, highly capitalized and often expatriate-dominated manufacturing industries with the workshops of small artisans in the city back streets. The dichotomy between modern and traditional, formal and informal sectors seems grounded in reality, however difficult a precise definition may subsequently prove to be. The dichotomy implies the dualist approach and raises the question of the relationship between the two sectors. For many economists the so-called informal or traditional sectors have been marginal in that they produced so little to swell the total Gross National Product (GNP). They are marginal also in that they are deemed to wither away, yet they show few signs of doing so. They are marginal in that the labour reserve contained within them has little consequence for wage rates and the working of the formal sector. The marginal sector is thus functionless for the dominant capitalist economy. Such approaches are now challenged by those who see a high degree of interdependence between the two sectors. The activities of small artisans, petty traders and the like are not oriented exclusively towards the poor; most of them draw their raw materials from the formal sector, and many sell their products and wares to this same sector, or to the wealthier classes. The linkage between the two forms of activity is complex; Marxists debate whether one should talk about several modes of production existing within the city and of the articulation between them, or whether one should see all as embraced within a single mode of production, termed perhaps that of dependent capitalism. The view that capitalism is not merely a modern accretion, but pervades the whole society, is gaining acceptance. And thus whilst liberal writers have rejected the thesis of the cultural marginality of the urban poor, the term marginality has been taken over by radicals who use it to designate the process whereby the poor are excluded from most of the benefits of modern urban life.

Within the radical camp, however, the use of marginality by some has brought them into conflict with their ideological peers who remain loyal to the terminology of class. Quijano (1972, 1974) has tried to resolve this conflict in defining a true proletariat – the wage earners with moderate incomes, steady employment and unionized, and a marginal proletariat – the badly paid, irregularly employed; there is too a petty bourgeoisie – the fairly well-off artisan or trader, and a marginal petty bourgeoisie – the grossly underemployed artisan, the street-hawker. But as he realizes, these economic distinctions are not replicated in social groupings. In fact a man may be a wage labourer by day, a petty trader by night; a variety of occupations are found within the family; a wage employee aspires to become a small independent entrepreneur. Furthermore, not only does the marginal proletariat live side by side with the marginal petty bourgeoisie, but they are frequently not dissimilar in number. A social homogeneity masks the diversity of economic categories and interests.

Boundaries between marginal and non-marginal, whether in terms of people or occupations, are fuzzy. But in the housing sphere the distinction is magnified; for as we have seen the urban population is divided clearly into those who can afford a house on an estate, obtaining a mortgage to purchase it, and those who live in rented accommodation in the inner-city slums or who have begun to build their own homes in a pueblo joven. The resident on the housing estate may easily sell his house and move to a better one as he prospers economically; for the poblador of the pueblo joven this, as we shall see, is not possible.

The small pueblo joven thus tends to develop certain highly significant characteristics. On the one hand the density of interpersonal relation-ships, kinship and marriage, co-godparenthood, long co-residence as neighbours and as co-workers in many co-operative enterprises, gives the little community the density and cohesion of a stereotypical village. On the other hand the lack of common economic interests and the wide range of incomes which develop over the years tend to impede collective action. This is important inasmuch as government policy focuses upon the pueblo joven as the effective unit of social improvement and popular mobiliza-tion. The failure of such policies contributes to the increased 'margina-tion' of the poor.

The following chapters explore these themes in more detail. I first give a very brief outline of Peru and its people stressing both the continuing distinctiveness of Indian and Spanish cultures and the relatively slow rate of economic development. This development has produced a great mi-gratory flow towards Lima in particular, a flow in which the migrant Indian from the sierra and the Spanish criollo culture of the city confront each other. I shall then look more closely at the rapid growth of Lima in recent decades and show how the housing policies adopted by the gov-ernment were quite inadequate for the rate of migration; the migrant poor were forced to seek their own solution in the creation of peripheral squalid settlements. These barriadas house the poor, though their resi-dents are not much poorer than those who remain in the inner-city slums and 'convencional' housing of the lower strata. A statistical over-view of these settlements, however, obscures the diversity both between them and within any one of them.

To exemplify the latter I give an ethnographic description of one small settlement. Two features emerge from this description: firstly, the settle-ment is in many respects an isolated community, rather like a village; but is it really a community and what are its characteristics as a community? I explore this theme by looking at the collective action that is undertaken within the settlement. Secondly, the people of the settlement are in many ways integrated into city life; examples of this integration will be provided in the ethnographic chapter. In a chapter on marginality I take this concept and examine the way in which, variously defined, it illuminates the relationship of the small settlement and its peoples to the city and state.

This analysis leads to two apparently contradictory findings. On the one hand the degree of cultural and economic integration of the pobladores of the pueblo joven is high. Yet the form which urbanization has taken in Lima seems to be dividing its population into two distinct worlds: that of the pueblos jóvenes and that of the 'regular' suburbs. The polarization of these two is increased by certain processes – for example the lack of territorial mobility between the two – and mitigated by others – for example the development of large pueblos jóvenes into self-governing municipalities.

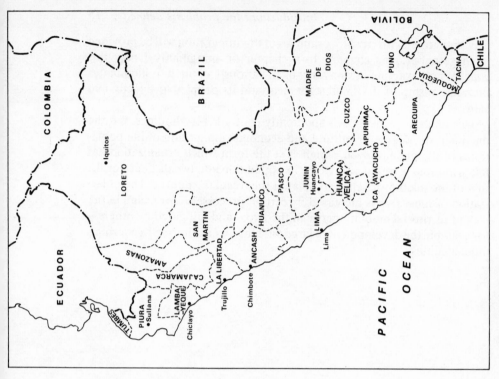

1 Peru: physical

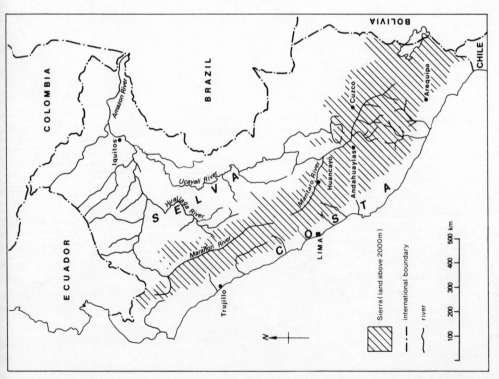

2 Peru: departments

2. Peru: land and people

Peru is a vast country. Its area of just over three-quarters of a million square kilometres equates it with West Germany, France and the Iberian peninsula. Its northernmost border almost touches the equator, its southern tip is at 18° S latitude; the Pacific coastline extends for 2,250 kilometres. Yet it is a sparsely populated country; the present population is only 14,000,000, but that is five times the population recorded in the census of 1876 and over double that of 1940. With a present annual growth rate of nearly 3 per cent the population will double every 25 years.

The country is conventionally divided into three zones each of which, in its own way, presents an inhospitable environment to man. The *costa* (the narrow coastal plain and the western slopes of the Andes up to a height of 1,950 metres) is 11 per cent of the total area of Peru; the *sierra* (the Andes mountains above 1,950 metres) accounts for 26 per cent of the area; and the *selva* (the eastern slopes of the Andes and the Amazon headwaters) makes up the remaining 63 per cent. In 1961 a third of the population lived on the costa (three-quarters in towns), 56 per cent in the sierra and only 11 per cent in the selva; the sierra proportion has, in fact, been declining because of migration to the coastal sugar estates, mining centres and towns and, to a lesser extent, to newly opened agricultural areas in the selva.

The costa is desert. The on-shore winds, which blow across the cold northward-flowing Humboldt current, rise when they meet the Andes to produce a low bank of cloud which depresses the temperature 10° C below that which is normal in such latitudes; rain almost never falls below an altitude of 1,500 metres, though the cloud on reaching ground level produces a damp mist. Sand dunes cover much of the coastal plain; the equally arid Andean slopes are deeply carved by erosion. Some fifty rivers drain into the Pacific but most of these rise in the easternmost ranges of the mountains; their flow is seasonal. Yet these rivers permit the irrigation of the coastal valleys and the growing of maize and rice as staples, sugar and cotton as export crops.

The Andes are one of the world's most dramatic mountain ranges. Peru's highest peak, Mount Huascarán, rises to over 6,600 metres. Parallel ranges impede penetration from the coast; both road and railway, eastward from Lima to La Oroya, the mining centre, and thence to the selva and to Huancayo, the new capital of the fertile Mantaro valley, climb to over 4,500 metres. Such valleys, their rivers mostly draining to the Amazon, lie at altitudes between 2,400 and 3,600 metres, the rivers often cutting deep gorges. Movement between valleys is difficult. In each, the level land is intensively cultivated and many of the hillsides are terraced; limited irrigation exists. Maize is the staple crop at lower levels, potatoes at higher altitudes. Above these valleys is the *puna*, the bleak plateau which sustains a vegetation of rough perennial grasses and shrubs, useful only for the grazing of sheep and llama.

The eastern slopes of the Andes are wetter (within a rainfall exceeding 250 centimetres annually) and hotter. In the high selva, or *montaña*, tropical cash crops – tea, coffee, cocoa – are now grown. The low selva, the valleys of the Amazon tributaries, is thick, impenetrable jungle. Although the low selva comprises half of the country, it has remained neglected for centuries. Its indigenous people, perhaps numbering a million today, are Indians who remained largely unaffected by Incaic and pre-Incaic cultures; they live in small isolated groups with a very simple technology.

Historical background

The Indian peoples of Peru probably arrived in the country 10,000 or more years ago, though until 3000 B.C. they were a hunting, fishing and food-gathering people. Following the development of agriculture small states were created, the urban centres being dominated by the pyramidal temples. The Chavín culture, which is one of the best known of the pre-Incaic cultures, is associated with a site in the Huaylas valley in the northern sierra. The classic period, which saw the florescence of city-states with most artistic pottery and textiles, spanned the years A.D.200–600. By the end of the millennium these polities were fragmented and engaged in warfare.

The Inca emerged onto the historical stage in about A.D.1200. The founder of the dynasty established his little kingdom at Cuzco and in the ensuing 200 years his successors conquered the near-by territory. In a period of phenomenal expansion between 1438 and the death of Huayna Cápac in 1527 the Inca established an empire which extended 4,800 kilometres through the sierra from what is now Ecuador to central Chile, embracing an area of some half a million square kilometres and an estimated population of 6,000,000. Sierra and costa were united in a single polity, but the selva remained beyond the limits of this empire.

Inca conquest undoubtedly allowed the many small agricultural communities to continue to live and work in a traditional manner. Nevertheless a rigid and intricate hierarchical system of administration enabled a surplus to be extracted from the peasantry to maintain officials, armies and the masons who built the impressive array of stone palaces, temples and forts in Cuzco itself and in near-by imperial outposts.

The empire's collapse was even more swift than its creation. At Huayna Cápac's death the throne passed to his elder son who ruled at Cuzco; his favourite son Atahualpa was given the northern part of the empire. The latter procured the assassination of his brother and then he was himself lured into captivity by Francisco Pizarro and his little force of 200 Spaniards and subsequently executed. Pizarro reached Cuzco in 1533.

The following years witnessed a limited resistance by the Indians, rivalry between the *conquistadores*, and their reluctant submission to rule by imperial officials from Spain. Yet the speed with which Spanish dominance was effected seems remarkable, though the booty of Inca gold undoubtedly intensified interest in the country.

Lima then became the capital of an extensive viceroyalty. In the interior, a series of provincial centres was developed, each with its grid pattern of streets and its main square flanked by an imposing church. In Cuzco many of the new public buildings were constructed on Incaic foundations. In such a system, individual settlements were ultimately linked to Lima; but relations between units of equivalent status were tenuous and weak. For the peasant, Spanish rule meant taxation, collected by Spanish officials and their Indian intermediaries, and the recruitment of labour for the silver mines at Potosí in the south of the state. Under this latter system, described as heir to the Incaic collective labour or *mita*, no more than one-seventh of the adult male population was supposed to be taken from a community at any one period; this rule was certainly breached. The Spanish brought to their territory new techniques such as the plough and iron tools; they also introduced the horse, mule and donkey, as well as cattle. Mission influence was ubiquitous, though many small communities saw a priest only once a year.

In the early decades of the nineteenth century the locally born or creole Spanish revolted, as had the North American colonists, against rule from Europe and, following the successful campaigns of Simón Bolívar, San Martín and other soldiers, Peru was created on 28 July 1821. The change in political leadership did not, however, result in any equally dramatic change in the economy of the country nor in the social life of its people.

During the nineteenth century the haciendas increased in scale and power with the development of the wool trade. Any image of the hacienda as a large productive estate, geared to the maximization of profit, is erroneous. It is estimated that 1,000 families owned 60 per cent of the total arable land of the country. But many of the biggest estates comprised vast areas of extensively grazed pasture at high altitudes. The haciendas were worked by the labour of men who lived either on the estate, perhaps working half of their time on the estate land and half on their own plots, or by men who lived in traditional communities. The dominant image is of a landowner who has his peons at his beck and call, for both agricultural and domestic services. At one extreme an absentee owner might leave his estate in the care of a manager, ruthless and cruel to his workers; at the other, a benign paternalism existed. The image of the wealthy *gamonal* (owner-manager or overseer) riding around his estate, his horsewhip and pistols conspicuous, contrasts with that of the poor *hacendado* (farm owner), living in a style little above that of his workers. The scale of hacienda ownership contrasts with the fact that 60 per cent of rural labour worked its own small plots – the *minifundios* – and produced here a substantial proportion of the foodstuffs consumed within the country.

Conventionally, the population of Peru has been classed as Indian, mestizo and white. The Indians comprise about half the total; Peru, and Bolivia too, are unique among South American states in having such a large proportion of their population identifying with traditional rather than Spanish culture. The terms are, however, social categories, and can vary according to context; thus a man might be viewed as a mestizo in his home village, but an Indian when he is in Cuzco. In the southern sierra, the heartland of the Inca empire – the *mancha india* – over four-fifths of the population is Indian; in the north the proportion is much lower.

'Indianess' is characterized by the speaking of Quechua or Aymara, and by residence in a traditional community. Correlates include poverty, subsistence agriculture, distinctive dress, the chewing of coca. Until recently Quechua had not been recognized as an official language, and had not been taught in schools. The rural Indian learned little or no Spanish and was debarred from participation in national life. In the traditional community, or *ayllu*, some 5,000 of which are now recognized, the Indians are closely related by ties of common descent; land is allocated according to communal rules, some of it being for collective pasture, some to be worked by all for the support of priest or office-holders. Indigenous religious beliefs and practices continue beneath the thin veneer of Roman Catholicism.

At the opposite end of the social scale are the whites, said to number some 10–15 per cent of the population. These include descendants of the early Spanish colonists, few of whom could now deny the existence of some Indian blood in their veins, for unions between the conquistadores and Inca princesses were common. Later migrants from both Mediterranean and north European countries are likely to be of purer stock. Together, the wealthier families of these categories comprise the national oligarchy, dominating the social life of Lima.

Between Indian and white are the mestizos, those of mixed blood. Socially too they are an intermediate, though ill-bounded category. In the rural and predominantly Indian areas the mestizo is the small hacendado, the trader and clerk; he is politically and economically dominant in local society. The tension and hostility existing in his relationship with the Indian is manifest in an exaggerated respect for a Spanish way of life, the material conditions of which are often difficult to attain. In rural areas where mestizos predominate, Spanish is universally spoken. In urban society all those ranked below the dominant white oligarchy are mestizos.

The dichotomy between urban and rural society is characterized by the terms 'criollo' and 'serrano', describing not persons, but behavioural traits. 'Criollismo' is shrewdness, guile and resourcefulness in contrast to the dour stolid simplicity of the serrano peasant Indian. Criollo traits are found on the coast and especially in the cities, and imply an adaptation to urban life; they enhance the cultural distinctions between mestizo and Indian.

The Indian who breaks free from his traditional community, working in mines, on plantations or as a city labourer, quickly learns Spanish; he may even deny an ability to speak Quechua; he discards distinctively Indian dress for the universal suit or shirt and slacks. But he remains closely tied to his home community, perhaps retaining land rights there. As we have seen above, he is the cholo; this is a term used as one of endearment between such social equals but of abuse when an employer sees his Indian employee to be rising above his station, with an aggressive assertion replacing the expected docile obedience. The cholo is the urbanized Indian though, as with other terms described, its usage varies widely according to context.

Other racial groups complete the Peruvian population. Negro slaves were imported by the Spanish colonists to work on coastal plantations in the absence of Indian labour, and as preferred domestic servants. Negro communities have continued to exist with relatively little miscegenation, though African cultural traits have almost completely vanished. Negroes now number 35,000, almost half of them living in Lima. Chinese were brought in the mid-nineteenth century to work on the guano deposits on the off-shore islands and on railway construction; Japanese came later as entrepreneurs. Together these orientals number about 30,000, most now living in Lima where many are engaged in small-scale commerce. Finally there are those recent European or North American immigrants, residing semi-permanently in the country and in many cases well on the way to full assimilation into Peruvian society.

Contemporary political development

After Independence the tightly interwoven families of the conservative white oligarchy continued to dominate Peruvian life, though the occasional mestizo rose to political prominence. But landholding groups have yielded political power to an elite entrenched in industry and finance, though the distinctions have become blurred as many haciendas were in fact held by Lima-based corporations, rather than a local provincial gentry.

Radical ideas in Peruvian politics developed in the 1920s. Jóse Carlos Mariátegui, an upper-class intellectual, was educated in France where he came under communist influence; his essays on the 'reality of Peru', published in 1928 and frequently reprinted, have influenced subsequent generations of revolutionary intellectuals, though the communist party which he helped to form has remained relatively weak. The main threat to the political domination of the oligarchy came from the American Popular Revolutionary Alliance, usually known as APRA, founded in the 1920s by Víctor Raul Haya de la Torre. Although starting with *indigenista* goals, the party found its support mainly among city wage earners and the workers on the coastal sugar plantation. It attracted, too, liberals from the upper classes. At certain periods the party was opposed by severe repression and it was prevented from attaining electoral victories. In attempts to achieve office in the post-war period, Haya de la Torre allied his party with oligarchic factions and so became discredited in the sight of many members who turned to more radical and more fragmented revolutionary groups. The party came to be seen as being quite conservative, standing to the right of more liberally Christian and democratic groups, still of predominantly upper-class membership.

In the 1978 elections for a Constitutional Assembly which marked the beginning of the return to civilian rule, APRA emerged as the largest single party with a third of the votes. It still retains its ambiguous image and exploits this in attempting to win support from radical groups whilst not antagonizing the business community.

None of these political parties made any concerted attempt to reach the rural population, many of whom in any case lacked the franchise. During the 1950s, however, peasant uprisings increased in strength. In many cases intellectuals from Lima sought to provide leadership; though with their abstractly formulated goals they usually received little support from peasants who merely sought more land or a relaxation of hacienda exactions. The rising tension in the rural area, stimulated by the reforms promised by President Belaúnde, led the military government of 1968 to place land reform at the head of the policies. This military government has radically changed the political scene; for this, as we shall see, was no simple substitution of an aristocratic politician. The army itself has proved to be one of the main avenues of upward mobility for the mestizo; and General Juan Velasco Alvarado who led the military coup of 1968 was himself a man of humble origins.

Senior officers received an intensive training in social and economic sciences at the country's leading military academy. The army had been involved, in the previous decade, not only in crushing rural guerrilla movements but in rural reconstruction; in both capacities it had lived close to the rural masses. The new military rulers announced programmes of radical – or as they termed them, revolutionary – reform. Foreign-owned industries were to be nationalized; local industry was to be co-owned by its workers in 'industrial communities'; forms of co-operative enterprise were to be fostered as 'social property'. The expropriation of the haciendas, proposed by the previous civilian government but not carried out, was the prime element of land reform. Quechua was officially recognized and was to be taught in all schools, though the lack of teachers and texts and the multiplicity of dialects frustrated progress. Ministers wore the *poncho* when touring the sierra. In these and similar measures the regime aimed to restore the social dignity of the Indian – indeed to eradicate the racially based social divisions – and to destroy the overt dominance of the oligarchy, particularly in the social life of the country. In stressing nationalistic and populist themes and the social ownership of property, it aimed to obscure class-based divisions in society and to quell the militancy of the urban working class and the rural radical peasant movements. Outsiders have described the government as hovering uncertainly between the preservation of private property and a full-scale social transformation implied by its rhetoric (Lowenthal 1975).

The economically buoyant years of the early period of military rule were followed by ones of severe recession. The anchovy harvest failed, the new wells in the Amazon basin did not yield the expected quantities of oil, the nationalized iron mines were impeded in the marketing of their product. These established export industries thus failed to produce the foreign currency needed to service the massive debts which the government had incurred setting up its own spectacular new projects. Inflation rapidly increased, reaching 40 per cent a year in 1977. In a peaceful coup General Morales Bermúdez replaced Velasco in August 1975 and his government has pursued more conservative economic policies, relying more heavily on foreign aid and investment, and placating local businessmen by halting reforms in the spheres of social property and industrial community. Less money has been available for social services. The increasingly restive demands of the trade unions have been met with repression.

Economic development and inequalities

Marked social inequalities existed both in the pre-Incaic and Inca empires and in the Spanish colonial period. They continue to exist today – but with a difference. As never before men are able to migrate to seek new opportunities and social advancement; they have greater knowledge of new forms of employment; travel is easier; and legal constraints on movement have vanished.

Today, Peru is a typical underdeveloped country. A few products account for almost all exports, and the production of these is largely controlled by foreign or multinational firms. The earlier dominance of Britain in development at the turn of the century has been replaced by that of the United States. By 1968 'three-quarters of mining, half of fishing, two-thirds of sugar capital and half the cotton and wool processing plant were under foreign enterprise – which gave control over perhaps two-thirds of exports' (Fitzgerald 1976, p. 20). This foreign control was achieved in conjunction with Peruvian capitalists as local managers or financiers. Fitzgerald states that in 1968 one could identify six main ownership groups – groups of Peruvian families – which with their interests spread through mining and manufacturing, agriculture and banking, controlled some 70 per cent of the sales of the larger industries.

Let us look at some of these activities.

Sugar was introduced to Peru by the Spaniards and was, until the 1920s, the principal export crop. Some of the largest plantations have been located in irrigated areas of the northern coastal plain between the towns of Chiclayo and Trujillo. The plantation owners also controlled the processing plant and so dominated the production of the smaller growers. The larger estates are very efficient and yields per acre are relatively high. A typical estate might employ 200 permanent workers and 100 seasonal labourers (Sarfati Larson and Eisen Bergman 1969, p. 161).

Cotton is indigenous to the country but was not cultivated on a large commercial scale until the present century. Cultivation is concentrated, again in the irrigated coastal plain, in the Piura department in the north and Lima and Ica in the centre. It became Peru's leading export in the period 1920–60; in 1972 an estimated 100,000 persons were engaged in some aspect of cotton production.

One of Peru's earliest exports was guano, deposited over centuries on off-shore islands by sea-birds feeding on the anchovy. It was used as a fertilizer in pre-Inca times but was commercially exploited only in the mid-nineteenth century. However, over-exploitation has killed the trade. The wealth from the sea – the anchovy that thrive in the cold Humboldt current – continues to be harvested. Since 1945 the anchovy have been caught and processed into fish-meal, Chimbote becoming a leading centre; the meal is exported for animal feed. Variations in the ocean current can, however, drastically reduce the catch. Peruvian fishermen also catch tuna and bonito, and the country is, in terms of tonnage caught, the world's foremost fishing nation. Fish and fish-meal constituted over a quarter of the country's exports in the late 1960s.

The mineral wealth of the Peruvian sierra was one of the greatest attractions to the Spanish conquistadores; but gold and silver have now been replaced in importance by copper, iron, lead and zinc. Mines are located in the central sierra at high altitudes and often in inaccessible areas. The Cerro de Pasco Corporation has its vast lead and zinc refinery at La Oroya, east of Lima. In 1960, exploitation of the rich copper deposits began at Toquepala in the extreme south of the country; the iron mines of Marcona also in the southern costa began operation in 1953. Petroleum has been exported for several decades at Talara, on the northern coast; until the 1960s Peru was South America's chief producer. Recently, active exploration of the Amazon has revealed new fields, though perhaps not as rich as had been hoped. In the late 1960s copper rivalled fish products as Peru's most valuable export, and minerals, in their entirety, amounted to half of the country's exports.

Both sugar plantations and mines have recently been nationalized, but the ownership change has had little effect on production processes. The mining industry relies increasingly on skilled labour and though the areas of new exploitation offer foci of employment, in the older areas the demand for unskilled labour declines.

In 1940, Peru had relatively little manufacturing industry, in comparison with other South American countries. A series of favourable factors had produced strong stirrings in the 1890s but adverse factors subsequently halted this progress. The growth of the export trade in primary products militated against local investment in import-substituting industries. In 1923 'establishments manufacturing cotton, wool, flour, soap, candles, matches, cigars, shoes, hats and other consumer goods employed more than 30,000 workers' (Sarfati Larson and Eisen Bergman 1969, p. 104) in Lima. As in other underdeveloped countries, manufacture expanded rapidly only after 1945. Thus the contribution of manufacturing industry to the GNP of Peru rose from 16 per cent in the early 1950s to 22 per cent in the early 1970s. In fact the rate of growth of larger industrial concerns was greater than these figures suggest; figures for employment in 'manufacturing' included both those in larger firms and the small-scale artisan; the latter vastly outnumbered the former in the proportion 4:1, though the output per man in the larger firms was between 5 and 10 times that of the artisan. Of the 79 largest companies, responsible for half the sales and fixed assets, yet employing only 15 per cent of the workforce, only 20 were completely Peruvian-owned in 1968, while 41 were fully foreign-owned. Major enterprises included the iron and steel plant at Chimbote, inaugurated in 1958, and shipbuilding at Callao. But, as we shall see later, most of the light industry is concentrated in Lima. Thus of the 262 textile factories registered in 1956, employing nearly 24,000 people and constituting one of the larger single industries,

233, employing three-quarters of the workers, were located in Lima (Sarfati Larson and Eisen Bergman 1969, pp. 151, 152; Fitzgerald 1967, p. 12).

In contrast with those expanding sectors of the economy, the contribution of agriculture to the GNP has steadily declined. In mid-century many hacienda owners did endeavour to improve their techniques and invest in their estates. These changes, however, often resulted in a reduced demand for local labour. With the increasing threats of expropriation during the 1960s either under the proposed land reform measures or because of invasion by militant peasants, many hacendados left the farms and moved into the cities, reinvesting or living off their realizable assets. The estates which have now passed into public ownership continue to be run substantially on the pre-established lines and agrarian reform has done little to create new employment in the rural area. In fact migrants and others with tenuous legal rights to estate land have often lost them in favour of locally resident *comuneros*. Again, reform has not increased the area available to the independent peasant as minifundios – yet the population increases, and in costa and sierra little or no agricultural land remains to be brought under cultivation save through increased irrigation. It is the high selva or montaña which remains for development and here the new plantations of tropical and semi-tropical fruits attract the migrant.

The above catalogue of economic developments highlights both the recency of the changes, and the growing importance of the coast. The country is still very poorly served by internal transport. In the latter part of the nineteenth century the railway was built from Lima to La Oroya and Huancayo, a remarkable engineering feat; but whilst it certainly benefited the mining industries of that area, it contributed little to the agricultural development of the Mantaro valley, both because of the absence of feeder roads and because of the dominance of minifundios; large estates, had they predominated in this area, might have taken more advantage of the new link with the city. A second and longer railway links Cuzco with Arequipa and the sea; this line, though important for the local area and for Bolivia, carries only half the freight of the Lima–Huancayo line.

Only a tenth of Peru's 48,000 kilometres of road are paved, and most of the remainder are of unpaved earth, passable only in dry weather. The Pan-American Highway, running the full length of the Pacific coast and close to the sea, accounts for over half of the paved road; good roads link Lima with Huancayo and the selva towns of Tarma and Tingo María. But the sierra road from Huancayo to Cuzco and Puno, linking the several departmental capitals, is unpaved. In the 1960s plans were laid for a selva road running along the eastern Andean slopes, but little has been done to implement this. In the Amazon valleys the river is the most used route of communication. Yet though the Peruvian road system remains poor, the traffic has increased markedly in the past three decades: between 1930 and 1957 the number of cars registered increased eight-fold, buses and lorries ten-fold.

A poor transport system inhibits the spread of ideas as well as of goods; furthermore, the hacienda owners were not anxious to educate their workers. Thus, until very recently, illiteracy was widespread in the rural areas. In 1940, in the six southern sierra departments, between 72 per cent and 88 per cent of the adults were illiterate. Tullis (1970, ch. 6) describes graphically how an estate worker with a little experience of the world beyond would try to establish a little school for his own and other children; and how the hacendado might perhaps encourage him but could equally well frustrate his efforts. A concerted national effort to expand primary education throughout the country was beginning in the presidency of General Odría (1948–56); in the decade of the 1960s enrolments in primary schools doubled. More dramatic was the increase in secondary-school enrolment: three-fold in the same decade and ten-fold between 1950 and 1972. Yet in 1969 the number in primary schools was five times that in secondary schools; the latter were heavily concentrated in Lima and in provincial towns and thus provided few opportunities for the rural dweller. Again, over half of the 90,000 university students were enrolled in Lima.

Peru shares with other Latin American countries a most unequal distribution of income, and one, furthermore, which is more inegalitarian than in most developing nations. The bottom 20 per cent of the population receive only 3.5 per cent of the income, the bottom 60 per cent only 18.2 per cent, whilst the top 10 per cent receive 49.2 per cent.

The pattern of distribution in 1961 by occupation, regions and sectors is shown in Table 1.

Table 1 corroborates the picture given of the preponderance of modern economic development in the costa and in particular in the cities. The costa has only a third of the country's population yet generates well over half its income; the three-fifths who live in the sierra provide two-fifths of the income. And of the income produced in the sierra one-seventh returns to Lima as interest and rent. In half of the sierra provinces, the average per capita income in the early 1960s was below S/.6,000 annually; in none of the costa provinces did it fall so low. Three-quarters of the costa provinces had average means above S/.10,000; only one in nine in the sierra reached this level.

The figures for the costa as a whole mask the predominant position of Lima. This city alone accounts for over 20 per cent of the national population and over 40 per cent of its urban population. In 1961 its people received more than 40 per cent of the national income. Two-fifths

TABLE 1.   *Income distribution in Peru**

	Under S/.3,200	S/.3,201 –S/.7,000	S/.7,001 –S/.14,400	Over S/.14,401	Total labour force in 000s	Average Annual Income in S/.000
Total	25%	25%	25%	25%	3034	11.61
By occupational categories:						
sierra rural	51	28	14	7	1196	5.4
costa and selva farmers	4	13	33	50	196	16.2
wage earners (*obreros*)	7	34	34	25	747	11.1
white collar (*empleados*)	–	7	19	74	350	30.2
urban self-employed	14	27	33	26	476	12.6
By regions:						
all rural	38	31	19	12	1735	7.3
all urban	6	19	33	42	1299	19.5
Lima	4	13	29	54	619	23.3
mancha india	51	21	14	14	750	7.4
By section:						
modern	–	4	26	70	587	30.2
traditional urban	10	30	39	20	792	10.9
traditional rural	46	25	16	13	1392	11.7

* This table (adapted from Webb 1977, and some earlier presentations of similar data) divides the total Peruvian labour force into quartiles and then shows the proportion of each category which falls into each quartile. Thus 51 per cent of the sierra farmers fall into the bottom quartile earning below S/.3,200 annually, and only 7 per cent fall into the top quartile earning more than S/.14,400.

of government employees work in the capital, 70 per cent of those in large manufacturing industries.

The poverty and stagnation of the rural areas (particularly in the sierra), the opportunities presented by the new enterprises on the coast – the plantations, mining centres and fisheries – and the centralization of so much manufacturing industry and commerce, financial activity and administration in Lima itself, all set the scene for a description of migration patterns.

Migration

The population of Peru was relatively mobile in the Incaic period and also in Spanish colonial times with the redistribution of agricultural labour and the recruitment to the mines. But today the movement is much greater. In 1961 the national census recorded 23 per cent of the population living in a province other than that of birth. Of these almost 16 per cent had moved from one department to another, a figure which had grown from 9½ per cent in the 1940 census. By 1975 the inter-provincial movement had probably risen to a third of the total population.

The movements take a multitude of forms. They embrace both men and women; wives who have married across local boundaries, girls who have gone to the cities for domestic work. Migrants in this sense include the labourer who moves to a neighbouring hacienda in the adjacent province, the poor farmer who seeks wage employment in a near-by provincial town, as well as those who travel further afield to work on plantations or in the cities. And of course it is not only the poor who emigrate; children of the provincial elites, after a university education, find posts in the larger cities. The wealthier and better educated are more mobile than the poor.

In general the movement is away from the sierra. Almost all the sierra departments, according to the 1961 census, were rapidly losing people. In those of mancha india – Apurímac, Ayacucho, Huancavelica, Puno – and, too, in Cajamarca and Huánuco, immigration was minimal. In other departments a high rate of emigration was nearly balanced by immigration; thus, though Arequipa lost heavily, it was also receiving migrants from neighbouring backward Puno and to a lesser extent Cuzco. On the one hand the mines and plantations in the costa attracted wage labourers, on the other they also lost population, especially to Lima. In general the provincial centres attracted people from the adjacent departments rather than from further afield.

Of the 780,000 migrants resident in Lima in 1961 the following departments contributed more than 50,000 (the figures in brackets give the proportion of those born in that province who were in Lima): Ancash 88,000 (13.3 per cent); Ayacucho 73,000 (14.4 per cent); Arequipa 69,000 (16.9 per cent); La Libertad 68,000 (10.7 per cent); Junín 62,000 (11.6 per cent); Ica 51,000 (19.6 per cent). The departments of Tacna, Apurímac, Lambayeque and Pasco each had over 10 per cent of their natives in Lima alone. Piura and Cuzco, though sending over 40,000 people to the capital, lost only 6.3 and 4.9 per cent of their people respectively; in contrast, Puno lost only 1.9 per cent of its inhabitants to Lima (though this department is the principal supplier of migrants to Cuzco, Arequipa and Tacna).

There is also a reverse movement out of Lima. Youths born and educated there travel to the rural areas as teachers and clerks, as policemen and soldiers. City-born children of migrants return to their home areas. But such a flow is minimal in comparison with the immigration into Lima.

This movement may be expressed not only as a flow between regions but as a movement to the cities. In 1940 when Lima's population was only 645,000, Peru had nine other cities with populations of over 20,000: Arequipa 77,000, Cuzco 41,000, Trujillo 37,000, Iquitos 32,000, Chiclayo 32,000, Piura 28,000, Huancayo 27,000, Sullana 21,000 and Ica 21,000. In the ensuing two decades most of these towns grew at a rate above 4.0 per cent per annum, the exceptions being Cuzco and Iquitos. The smaller towns, mostly departmental capitals, had a noticeably slower growth rate – mostly between 2 per cent and 3 per cent – and barely above the rate of natural increase of the population. A few startling exceptions exist: Chimbote, centre of the fishing industry, grew from 4,000 to 60,000 in this period. In 1961 Peru had one city with a population over one million: Lima (1,800,000); two with over 100,000 inhabitants: Arequipa (162,000) and Trujillo (104,000); seven with between 50,000 and 100,000 people and sixteen with populations between 20,000 and 50,000. Expressed differently, the urban population of Peru rose from 35 per cent in 1940 to 47 per cent in 1961 and an estimated 51 per cent in 1967. (These figures are somewhat lower if the United Nations (UN) definition of an urban settlement – having a population over 2,000 – is used; the Peruvian census defines as urban a place with 'urban characteristics and functions': water, electricity, paved streets and an administrative centre.)

The rapidity of growth is reflected in the proportion of city residents living in the barriadas or spontaneous settlements whose mode of formation is described in the following chapter. In 1961 two-thirds of Chimbote's population was resident in barriadas; a proportion reflecting the small size of the town before 1940 and the consequent absence of 'inner-city slums'. Arequipa, Sullana, Chiclayo, Piura and Trujillo all had a third of their people in barriadas whilst in Lima, at this time, the proportion was relatively low (25 per cent). Cuzco – to give an example of a large but stagnant provincial capital – had only 6 per cent of its people in barriadas.

But let us now look more closely at the growth of Lima and examine the manner in which the barriadas of this city have developed in the past three decades.

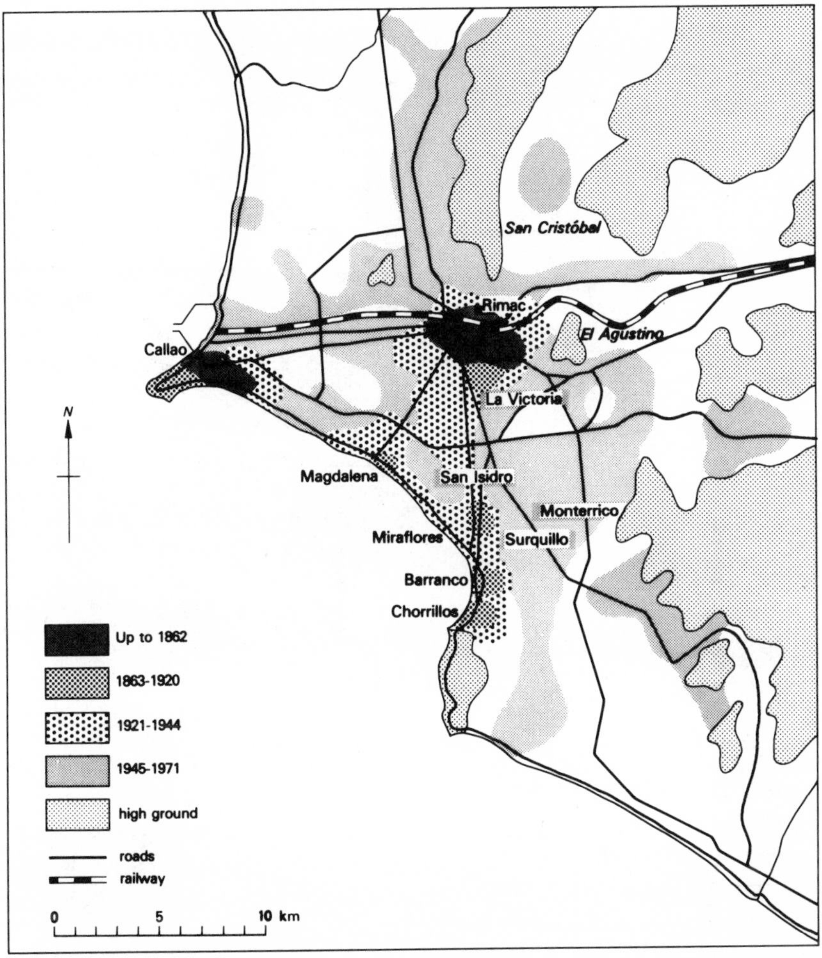
San Cristóbal
Rimac
El Agustino
Callao
La Victoria
N
Magdalena
San Isidro
Monterrico
Miraflores
Surquillo
Barranco
Chorrillos
Up to 1862
1863-1920
1921-1944
1945-1971
high ground
roads
railway
0
5
10 km

3 The growth of Lima

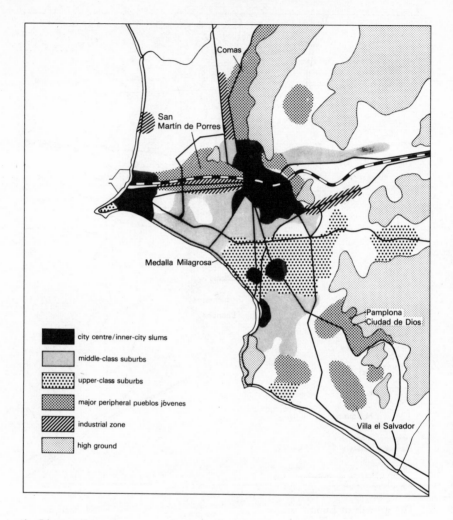

Comas

San
Martín de Porres

Medalla Milagrosa

Pamplona
Ciudad de Dios

Villa el Salvador

city centre/inner-city slums

middle-class suburbs

upper-class suburbs

major peripheral pueblos jóvenes

industrial zone

high ground

4   Lima: urban zones

3. Lima and the development of pueblos jóvenes

The growth of Lima

Dominant in this picture of migratory movement is the growth of Lima. A century ago only 5 per cent of the national population lived in the capital; now a quarter of the total population and one-half of the urban population lives in the metropolitan area. A roughly estimated half of the migratory movement is towards Lima.

In the sixteenth century Pizarro's capital had only 14,000 inhabitants. A census of 1614 recorded nearly 27,000, of whom half were Spaniards, 10,000 were negroes, 2,000 Indians and 1,000 mestizos. The city grew to 60,000 by mid-eighteenth century, but growth was slow thereafter with Peru's independence from the neighbouring states, previously part of her viceroyalty. The city had 100,000 inhabitants in 1876 and grew to 150,000 at the beginning of the present century. By 1930 the population of the metropolitan area (including Callao) had increased to a third of a million, and thereafter to half a million in 1940, $1\frac{1}{2}$ million in 1961 and an estimated $3\frac{1}{2}$ million in 1975 (Deler 1975, pp. 15–17).

The migrants to the cities have been young people, predominantly in their teens and early twenties; as a result gross urban birth-rates have been high. Thus it is estimated that, between 1940 and 1960, natural increase accounted for a little below a half of Lima's growth, just over a half being due to immigration. This means that in the period 1940–5 (allowing for some emigration) about 20,000 persons annually arrived in the capital; in the period 1956–60 this figure had risen to well over 50,000 (Deler 1975, p. 25).

A large part of Lima's population consists, of course, of children born in the city to recent immigrants, who are thus native to the city. Of the one million immigrants residing in Lima in the early 1960s an estimated 10.5 per cent had arrived before 1931, 12.7 per cent between 1931 and 1940, 23 per cent between 1941 and 1950, 32.7 per cent between 1951 and 1960 and 18.7 per cent between 1961 and 1965; thus approximately two-thirds had arrived in the two decades following the end of the Second World War.

The origins of these migrants have already been described. It is estimated that half have come from the departments of the sierra, 40 per cent from those of the costa. The definitions here used may, however, obscure the fact that many of the latter came not from coastal cities and planta-

33

tions but from mountain regions lying within the department. Much-quoted results of the 1961 census show that 7 per cent of Lima's immigrants come from cities with over 100,000 persons, 26 per cent from smaller cities of 20–100,000 inhabitants, 17.4 per cent from provincial towns of 5–20,000, 43.3 per cent from smaller settlements of 1–5,000, and 6.1 per cent from settlements with fewer than 1,000 people. It is pointed out that over 60 per cent of the total population live in settlements in this last category. It is thus argued that the migrants are not farmers but are urban workers before their arrival in Lima; a step migration is adduced from this. Uzzell states his belief that fewer than 20 per cent of the migrants were seen, culturally, as Indians on migrating, perhaps as little as 10 per cent; the majority were cholo or mestizo. Yet the same census figures show that almost 40 per cent of the migrants to Lima were previously working in agriculture. In the DESCO (Centro de Estudios y Promoción de Desarrollo) sample survey (Gianella 1970, p. 16) nearly two-thirds of the respondents were of rural origin; and four-fifths had come directly to Lima, not using other places as staging posts (Sarfati Larson and Eisen Bergman 1969, p. 136; Cotler and Laquian 1972, p. 113).

Surveys in the barriadas often show an even higher proportion of Lima's migrants coming from the sierra. Thus Matos Mar's census of the mid-1950s shows 61 per cent of the heads of families coming from the sierra provinces, Ayacucho and Ancash being the most heavily represented; of the 36 per cent who came from costa provinces, 15 per cent were from the Lima department itself, and two-thirds of these came from Lima province. It would seem likely that later data would show an even higher proportion of barriada residents of sierra origin. The discrepancy between these figures and those cited in the previous paragraph may arise from problems of definition of areas; it may be that migrants cite as their place of origin their district, rather than their hamlet, and so become recorded as native of a more urban settlement. It is also possible that the barriadas attract more strongly those of rural sierra origin, the urban migrant being better able to secure regular and well-paid employment, and thus afford to buy or rent adequate city accommodation.

Lima's growth is manifest in the growth not only of its barriadas but also of its residential suburbs. At the turn of the century Lima did not extend far beyond its original city walls. Expansion was mainly eastwards into the Barrios Altos, southward into La Victoria, and across the river to Rímac. In 1931, 200,000 people, well over half the city's population, lived in the central district or Cercado. Callao at that time had a population of 63,000. Miraflores (25,000), Barranco (14,000) and Magdalena del Mar (8,000) were the seaside resorts for the wealthier city residents. Much of the older property here has now fallen into decay; and Miraflores, in spite of its prestige and affluence, has its own adjacent slum areas of early origin. In recent decades there has been a rapid infilling of the area is that of San Isidro, though with the total infilling of this area and Magdalena del Mar have become suburbs with a predominantly *empleado* (salaried employee) population. The most wealthy residential area is that of San Isidro, though with the total infilling of this area high-class estates have more recently been built eastwards from Mira-flores towards Monterrico. The area between Lima and Callao is now occupied by modern industry. Estates of modest houses are now extending towards this area from Pueblo Libre and Magdalena del Mar, but this area – San Miguel – still has vacant land for building (Lewis 1973, p. 20).

The first barriadas were built, according to Matos Mar (1966) in the 1920s; before 1940 only 5 existed, and only 2 of these – Puerto Nuevo in Callao (pop. 6,000 in 1956) and Leticia on the slopes of San Cristóbal (pop. 2,800 in 1956) – were of any size. The earthquake of 1940, which destroyed much old man decaying property in Lima and Callao, precipitated the formation of 4 more. But the movement began to accelerate only after 1945. By the time of Matos Mar's survey in 1955 only 39 barriadas had been created, and these contained not more than 120,000 people – one-tenth of the population of the metropolitan area.

The early barriadas were built on the steep-sided slopes of the hills overlooking the city – San Cristóbal and El Agustino – and along the banks of the river Rímac between Lima and Callao. In 1956, half the barriada population lived in the latter area. The major directions of settlements in later years were firstly the barriadas running from the road northwards out of Lima into the steep dry valleys, the Carabayllo complex. Comas was founded in 1958, Pampa de Cuevas in 1960 and El Ermitaño in 1962; secondly, were the barriadas which were developed south of the city, along the Atocongo road and the Pan-American High-way. Ciudad de Dios was formed by invasion in 1954 but development in this area belongs to the 1960s. In May 1971 a massive invasion at Pamplona was thwarted by the government which, however, was obliged to create a new settlement – Villa el Salvador – on a site measuring 5 kilometres by 8 kilometres, situated 20–25 kilometres from the centre of Lima, but still adjacent to earlier barriadas. Its population reached 200,000 within 3 years.

By 1966 the number of barriadas had increased to 182 with a population of 437,000, 19 per cent of the total population of the metropolitan area; by 1970 this had increased to 273 and their population to 762,000, 26 per cent of the city. With the creation of new barriadas (e.g. Villa el Salvador), the extension of existing ones and the natural increase of the population it is estimated that the barriada population is already well over the million mark, and that by 1980, 40 per cent of Lima's population will live in such settlements.

The housing problem

The migrants came to Lima seeking work and needing accommodation. But the number of regular wage-earning jobs created annually falls far behind the flow of new applicants. The poor migrant, lacking both financial capital and a good steady income – for he has to make a living from casual work or in the informal economy – is unable to afford housing built to middle-class western standards.

Between 1949 and 1962 private builders constructed 62,200 houses in Lima; the public sector built 10,700. In the year 1960, 6,100 houses were built by the private sector, 380 by the public sector. In this year, as we have already seen, the population of Lima increased by approximately 100,000. Other figures for later periods give the same picture. Between 1949 and 1967, 112,000 houses were built by the public sector, 31,000 by the private sector. In 1966 it was estimated that 110,000 new houses would be needed annually in order to meet the existing shortage and future demands. The 5-year plan (1971–5) of the military government promised a total of 463,000 new units in this period, but only 8 per cent of these were expected to come from the public sector. The building of new houses by the state and by private contractors fails by a large margin to keep pace with the needs of the growing population and the continual deterioration of old housing (Harris 1963; Deler 1975, pp. 66–7; Aguirre 1974, p. 263).

The private sector includes a large number of small contractors, employing casual labour and working on one or two houses at a time. But it is dominated by large companies in which oligarchic families are tightly intermeshed. Much of the level land over which the middle-class suburbs of Lima have recently expanded was, until recently, irrigated farmland in large estates owned by landed families. Their conversion of these estates to building-land sometimes involved ploys of dubious legality. Allied with them are the cement manufacturing companies and construction firms, occasionally themselves subsidiaries of multinational corporations. Some of these housing-estate companies now control several thousand dwellings each. One of the leading businessmen in this field is said to be concerned with three building societies, ten urbanization projects, seven building-material companies, four construction companies and twenty-eight real-estate companies (Deler 1975, p. 89).

The development of private building was given a great boost in the 1960s with the rapid expansion of building societies. Membership of such associations grew from 11,000 in 1962 to 350,000 in 1970 and soon after to 500,000. The building society movement was advocated by Beltrán in the late 1950s; it was stimulated too by visiting US advisers and massive US loans helped to establish many of the individual associations (US Dept of Housing and Development 1971, p. 139).

Such activity has, of course, pushed up the prices of land and housing. A survey conducted by Rodríguez and others of DESCO, from a study of newspaper advertisements, showed that in the 27 years from 1940 to 1967, wages had increased 37 times, salaries 22 times; but the price of land and the rents of houses and flats had increased by over 70 times; the price of new houses had increased 44 times, of flats even more.

Most of the housing built during this period is, thus, for a moderately rich clientele, and is far beyond the means of the poor migrant. Harris (1963, pp. 587–8) states that in the early 1960s a two-bedroom house built by a private builder would have cost approximately S/.127,000; the building society would advance 80 per cent of this, leaving the mortgagee to find S/.25,000 from savings or short-term credit. A monthly payment spread over 20 years would amount (at 6 per cent interest) to S/.1,346; to be able to afford this, an income four times as great is assumed – S/.5,400. But the average wage of white-collar workers in modern industries and services at this time, was between S/.3,000 and S/.4,000 monthly. Thus, only the above-average salary earner would be able to afford such a modest house. Harris estimates that the cost of private housing in Lima in 1961 averaged nearly S/.1,000 per square metre.

Low-cost housing, too, falls beyond the reach of most. Harris (1963, pp. 584 ff.) shows that families with annual incomes between S/.9,600 and S/.30,000 could afford houses costing S/.15–60,000. Contemporary surveys indicated that only 29 per cent of the barriada families had incomes below S/.9,600. Yet in a scheme at Ciudad de Dios, prices for houses ranged between S/.354 and S/.857 per square metre, excluding the cost of land; an average unit of 50 square metres cost S/.20–22,000. Thus a further third of the barriada residents would notionally be excluded from purchase of this type of house (Harris 1963, p. 445). The DESCO survey cited above demonstrates that *c*. 1967 only 17 per cent of Lima's population would be able to buy an average house in Callao or the north-east parts of the city where prices were lowest. In comparison, the costs of constructing one's own house in a barriada are given later in this chapter.

The situation has not changed radically in the succeeding decade. As Dwyer (1975, pp. 237–8) reports, the Peruvian government with UN assistance launched a new organization in 1968 in order to develop new techniques of low-cost housing. An international competition was organized for all Peruvian architects and thirteen foreign ones who were specially invited. This expensive competition was clearly not aimed at solving the problem of mass housing which concerns the urban poor, for the specifications indicated dwellings suitable rather for lower white-collar workers than for the inhabitants of Lima's pueblos jóvenes. Some of the schemes submitted involved the use of heavy machinery. Pilot schemes were instituted using several of these designs; but no large-scale scheme for the provision of very cheap houses has yet been undertaken.

Accommodating the poor

Apart from a number of experimental and pilot projects, the construction of new dwellings is aimed at the new middle classes. The private sector, for obvious reasons, builds for the rich, but the public sector, entrapped in its insistence to maintain 'acceptable' standards of building usually finds itself providing housing not for the very poor but for the relatively affluent, skilled worker in stable employment. It is, too, financially incapable of assuming the costs of a necessary housing programme. Deler (1975, pp. 66–7) argues that a public investment nearly six times as large as that of the late 1960s would be necessary if the state were to carry out its obligations.

For the poor there exist the houses vacated by the middle classes as they move from the inner-city areas to the newer suburbs, and the housing that they can provide for themselves as squatters. Whilst the barriadas claim the attention of politicians and scholars alike, it is over-looked that only one-third of the poor in the 1960s lived in such settlements; two-thirds lived in the inner-city slums of varying types (Gianella 1970).

In common with all large expanding cities, Lima has in its central areas decaying mansions of a departed bourgeoisie, now transformed into slum property of the worst type. Upkeep is minimal; staircases are dangerous, windows broken and covered with board or sacking. Large rooms are subdivided by flimsy partitions to create more units. Washing and toilet facilities are limited, dirty and shared by many families. Rents in 1975 might well have amounted to S/.1,800–S/.2,000 monthly for a single room when the statutory daily minimum wage was S/.118 giving a notional monthly income of S/.3,500 at best. In one recorded instance the landlord charged visitors S/.50 a night to sleep in a corridor. Such accommodation yields maximum insecurity, for not only is there a fear of eviction with temporary non-payment of rent, but the likelihood that the building will be condemned and the area redeveloped is very great.

Suffering equally from deterioration, but in a less spectacular fashion, are the areas of small property built in the first decades of this century: the suburbs of Rímac, Barrios Altos and La Victoria in particular. Not only are these buildings now crowded, but temporary structures of matting are often erected on their flat roofs. Patch (1967) has described the lives of some residents of the central market area, La Parada.

The callejones or alleys are purpose-built for the urban poor. These are found predominantly in the inner-city areas. They consist of a narrow passage opening on to the street, perhaps fronted, though not often, by an imposing gateway. On each side are arranged single or multiple rooms; their only light comes from windows facing the alley. A communal tap serves all needs. All social life takes place in the passage-way, which is usually festooned with laundry. The only full description of such a settlement again comes from Patch (1961). In an area measuring approximately 20 by 35 metres lived 30 families – 158 persons; one family whose breadwinner – a bricklayer – earned (in 1961) S/.42 a day paid a rent of S/.150 monthly plus S/.10 for light. Of the callejón's adult population half had been born in the sierra, two-fifths in Lima itself and the rest elsewhere on the coast. Both Lima- and sierra-born persons had lived, on average, for over 11 years in this settlement. Patch emphasizes the social disorganization produced by this mode of life: the marital disputes and irregular unions, the thieving by the young. Some degree of internal solidarity is shown by the repugnance of stealing within the settlement. The building of callejones ceased in the 1930s, partly because such single-storey structures were uneconomic in inner-city areas.

The corralón is a very different type of settlement. Throughout the residential area, single plots of land often remain underdeveloped. The owner may put a watchman on this land to safeguard his rights. With or without the knowledge of the landowner, other settlers are introduced. Frequently the watchman becomes the landlord, constructing in part the maze of dwellings – of mud, brick or waste-materials – which fill the plot. In terms of size and amenities the corralón is similar to the callejón. Eviction is a continuing threat, for the owner may decide to develop his land, or sell it to someone else who will. It seems likely however that fairly close bonds might exist between residents and the corralón's founder/landlord. Gavin Alderson-Smith (1975) describes how many of the migrants from the sierra village of Huasicancho settled in one small corralón in Petit Thouars in San Isidro; several of these migrants later moved out to more distant corralones or to barriadas when, as itinerant sellers of fruit and vegetables, they had achieved sufficient economic stability. The Petit Thouars corralón remained, however, a focus for the activity of the villagers.

In a recent survey of the central district of Lima nearly two-thirds of the slum population was located in callejones and a further fifth in decaying slum tenements; only 5 per cent lived in corralones, and 11 per cent in subdivided houses and other types of accommodation. In contrast, in Callao, 69 per cent lived in callejones and slum tenements and 21 per cent in corralones. The proportion of corralón dwellers is of course much higher in the residential suburbs; even wealthy San Isidro is reported to have 16 of them; in the older areas of Miraflores and of Magdalena del Mar they are most numerous (Deler 1975, p. 98).

Barriada formation

The formation of the barriadas has been the direct consequence of the lack of housing in the city, of the inability of state and private enterprise to build sufficient units to accommodate both migrants and the naturally increasing population. It is estimated that in the 1950s and 1960s barriada residents built as many houses as the private construction sector (Deler 1975, p. 66).

As we have seen, the experience of Peru differs in many respects from that of the other Third World countries. This is due to three factors. First, the inner-city slums – tenements, callejones, corralones etc. – have been able to house hundreds of thousands of migrants on their arrival in Lima. Second, the topography of Lima, and of other coastal towns too (uncultivated undulating desert expanses, and the lower slopes of Andean foothills) and the dry mild climate have favoured the seizure of large areas and the temporary settlement in most primitive housing. Third, the government, as will be detailed below, has acquiesced to this development and in relatively few instances has it resorted to the eradication of the new settlements.

Many of the smaller barriadas have developed by slow accretion. Labourers residing on or near agricultural land have invited friends and relatives to join them; building workers occupying vacant land near the construction on which they were working stay on and also invite others. In some respects the resulting settlements resemble a large corralón. But there are important differences: the founder settlers may charge an admission fee to later incomers but they are not landlords; all settlers enjoy squatters' rights and pay no rent. Unlike the corralón tenant they have the opportunity to build upon the land occupied.

The more spectacular process, however, is the invasion of land. A group of individuals living in the city meets secretly for several months to plan the invasion. Unfortunately no description of this process, nor of the characteristics of the members of such invading groups, has been made; scholars and government alike have been presented with a *fait accompli*. Yet it is clear that the invaders have lived for several years in the city. On the chosen night they descend suddenly upon the selected terrain, mark it out in regular plots, usually 20 metres by 50 metres, laying out spaces for streets and squares and erecting their own individual matting shelters. In a sample study of barriadas carried out by Collier (1976), half of the invaded land was publicly owned and only one-sixth was in undisputed private ownership; in the remaining cases the ownership of the private land was in dispute. A principal theme of Collier's study is the government's connivance in or acquiescence to such invasions, though the exact degree of involvement is often hard to define. The invaders are politically astute. They seek the support of influential political leaders, either inside the government or outside it, but always able to harass those in power. They choose an invasion date which will deter the government from violent reaction: public holidays, Christmas, the presence in the city of foreign conference delegates. They pronounce their support for the regime: the national flag is flown on the new huts, the settlement is named in honour of the president or his wife. In a third of the barriadas surveyed by Collier (and these tended to be the larger ones accounting for three-fifths of the people within his sample) the government is deemed to have authorized the settlement in advance. This was, however, different from the establishment of the settlement by the government as happened in the case of Villa el Salvador. The greater the degree of government authorization, the less were the police likely to act. In some cases an invasion was met with only a symbolic show of force by the police. Active police intervention and the eventual eviction of the invaders was more common when private land was involved; however the proportion of evictions varied widely from one government to another.

With the invasion secured, the barriada continued to grow, new plots on the margins continually being laid out. Given the availability of land, the process continues today. Thus in a survey of Cuevas it was found that just over half the residents had been members of the invading group; in Mariscal Castilla fractionally under a half; but only 8 per cent of the residents of El Agustino and 3 per cent of San Martín de Porres – barriadas both much closer to the city centre and of earlier formation – were original invaders (Cotler and Laquian 1971).

The typical barriada resident is in Turner's terms (1963, 1965, 1968a) a 'consolidator'. The newly arrived migrant, the 'bridgeheader', seeks accommodation near the heart of the city, for it is here that most opportunities for casual employment exist. This need takes priority over that for a home of his own, with modern amenities. But once he finds a relatively stable form of employment the contrast between the high rents which he pays and the opportunity to build his own house in the barriada makes him a potential invader. His move is thus a consciously planned one. Others, however, would seem to have moved to their present barriada sites much more precipitantly. Some were evicted forcibly from another barriada; allegations exist that wealthy property-owners have instigated invasions as a means, in part, of removing tenants from slums owned by them in the heart of the city, thus facilitating the redevelopment of the area with a considerably higher rental value (Collier 1976, p. 73). In fact the life-histories provided by the pobladores usually stress the threat or actual eviction; their choice lay between the alternatives of settlement in a barriada, or finding similar accommodation in an inner-city tenement or corralón.

A persistent obstacle to house-building is the lack of legal title to land. Successive governments have promised action but the award of titles fails to keep pace with new settlements. The official recognition of the barriada removes the threat of eviction but this is not sufficient to demonstrate the individual's rights over his own plot. Yet lack of title has not deterred the many thousands who *have* built substantial houses, perhaps hoping thereby that eviction is rendered less likely.

One of the characteristics of the barriada is the variation in house style, displaying both the whims of the owners and their affluence. Well-constructed two-storey cement-block houses are juxtaposed with rough shacks. Houses are built by family labour with the assistance of kin expert in the various aspects of construction; work proceeds spasmodically with the accumulation of savings or with opportunities to acquire materials at low prices. Few families could say how much their house has cost them; and official surveys have given no detailed estimate of the amount of investment in such property.

Matos Mar (1966, pp. 23–5) has given estimates of the costs of house-building in the late 1950s.

A house, or rather a shelter, made of flattened cans and drums, cardboard, sacking and waste timber could be constructed for S/.100. A more substantial shelter using *estera* mats, woven reed screens and wood from packing cases might cost S/.200 to S/.800. A house with mud and reed walls – the traditional house in Lima – and an estera roof could cost between S/.800 and S/.2,000. A fourth type of house with walls of mud block and either an estera or a mud and reed roof, the most common type in the barriadas in the 1950s, could be built for S/.2,000 to S/.8,000. A better house, with the front wall of fired brick and other walls of mud, with a similarly substantial roof, might cost between S/.8,000 and S/.10,000. Finally a house completely built of brick would cost from S/.10,000 to S/.13,000. The cost per square metre of brick houses with cement floors is S/.50; for those of mud block with earth floor S/.24. These figures may be compared with those cited above for houses built by private construction companies at the same period: S/.127,500 for a two-bedroomed house or S/.1,000 per square metre.

Government policies towards barriadas

As Collier (1976) describes in detail, the policies of the Peruvian governments since 1945 towards the growing barriada phenomenon have been lenient and permissive; many invasions were thwarted but the ruthless and wholesale eradication of settled populations, characteristic of so many other countries, has not been typical of Lima. Instead Peru has perhaps led the way in showing what can be achieved when the squatters are left to their own devices and given minimal encouragement. The policies appear progressive; they are, however, basically conservative ones.

General Manuel Odría came to power in 1948 at the head of a military government which aimed to restore a political stability threatened by the growing influence of APRA. In attempting to undermine the appeal of APRA to the urban poor, he initiated widespread wage increases, embarked on housing-projects and public-works programmes. Land invasions were tolerated and frequently Odría appeared to side with invaders against the private landlords. He, and more especially his wife, perhaps conciously modelling herself on Eva Perón, made repeated visits to barriadas, dispensing charity. This marked paternalism, derived perhaps from Odría's membership of a sierra hacienda-owning family, created strong ties of personal dependency between the president and the barriada-dwellers; significantly the issue of titles to land, or any other move which would have granted right to the settlers, rather than favours, do not appear in his policies. By stimulating urban employment and in permitting barriada formation Odría probably encouraged migration to the city. Such a policy favoured sierra hacienda owners, capitalizing their estates; but it ran counter to the interests of the export-oriented groups within the oligarchy who had originally supported Odría's accession to power.

In 1956 Odría was succeeded by the elected government of Manuel Prado, one of the most influential members of which was Pedro Beltrán, a leading member of the oligarchy and spokesman for urban capitalism in Lima; he had been in the forefront of the opposition to Odría in his final presidential years. Beltrán, equally opposed to APRA and just as mindful of mass popular support, stressed policies of *laissez-faire* economic liberalism, rather than the paternalism of Odría. Housing was seen as a solution to poverty; the theme of *casa propia* – a home of one's own – was widely disseminated. The efforts of the poor to raise themselves, to attain a middle-class way of life, were promoted as a countervailing force to the growing radicalism of the poor. Beltrán was one of the prime movers in the creation of building societies; his policies brought prosperity to the construction industry.

It was at this period that William Mangin, an American anthropologist whose Peruvian experience had begun with the Cornell project at Vicos, was studying Comas and other barriadas. Mangin has been the principal exponent of the desire for self-advancement among city migrants, emphasizing their political conservatism, and denying the prevalence of crime, violence, broken families and such symptoms of social disorganization which the works of Oscar Lewis have presented as universal in urban slums. At this time there was also a British architect, John Turner, who worked as an adviser in government housing agencies. Turner's advocacy of self-help as a means of solving the housing problem now extends far beyond Latin America and constitutes one of the major programmes currently in vogue.

Many of these policies were embodied in Law 13517, the Law of the *Barrios Marginales* (marginal neighbourhoods: a new name heralding a supposed new approach) promulgated in 1961. New invasions were banned, but existing settlements would be remodelled and titles to land issued. Squatters on public land would pay a symbolic purchase price for their rights; those on private land would pay higher sums to compensate the owners. The National Housing Corporation would lay out new sites with basic services; the settlers would then build their own houses; they would also pay for the services installed. Three such *urbanizaciones populares*, accommodating 20,000 people, were started, though their effect was minimal in that they were largely occupied by settlers from inner-city land.

The military government of Pérez Godoy which succeeded Prado saw itself as a mere caretaker. It did not aspire to mass popular support and was more active in resisting the continuing invasions. It did, however, set up a new housing association, the Junta Nacional de la Vivienda (JNV), a body co-ordinating existing institutions in formulating and implementing a general housing plan. Widespread surveys of barriadas were carried out prior to remodelling the settlements and issuing titles; basic services – water and drainage – were provided for many settlements. Barriada associations were encouraged. Loans were available to individuals to buy building materials. However, the impact of the activities of the JNV declined during the 1960s as it failed to obtain government support and funds for its ambitious programmes and as the hopes of the barriada residents themselves, stimulated by the widespread publicity given to the Law of the Barrios Marginales and the creation of the JNV, turned to frustration.

Fernando Belaúnde Terry, president 1963–8 and leader of the reformist Acción Popular party, was a professional architect; he seemed more interested in extravagant city planning than in barriadas. On the site of the racecourse in Jesús María he built the large San Felipe estate, with high-rise flats, a shopping centre, and recreation areas. Designed for 1,500 middle-class families, escalating costs made this development available, in fact, to the upper-middle classes. Squatters evicted by this project constituted the invaders of new barriadas. Belaúnde sought his support in the rural area, promising, but not implementing, projects of land reform. A new highway running along the western slopes of the Andes was planned. Belaúnde hoped that rural development would stem the migratory flow to the towns, thus easing the slum problem.

In 1968 the civilian government of Belaúnde fell in the coup of General Juan Velasco Alvarado. Though the military rulers have proclaimed their policies as 'revolutionary' they embody, in fact, the tendencies of previous decades. Self-help has again become the key theme with the recognition that a government's inability to implement over-ambitious programmes leads only to frustration. In the opening years of the regime the army was active in major construction works: in levelling streets in barriadas; in constructing a dual-carriage highway to Comas. In December 1968 the barriadas were renamed pueblos jóvenes (young towns) with the creation of a new organization, Organismo Nacional de Desarrollo de Pueblos Jóvenes (ONDEPJOV) which had the task of stimulating and co-ordinating community development. It was a high-powered body, responsible directly to the president and prime minister; among its leading members were Bishop Bambarén, the 'bishop of barriadas', Diego Robles, an architect once associated with DESCO, and Carlos Delgado, former Aprista (member of the APRA) and one of Peru's leading sociologists who, too, had actively promoted the ideals of self-advancement held by the poor. One of ONDEPJOV's tasks was to implement at a faster rate the issue of legal titles, these no longer being conditional upon the remodelling of the settlement.

For two years there were no new invasions of land. Then came the Pamplona invasion of May 1971 (Montoya 1973); the invaders were eventually resettled in the new pueblo joven of Villa el Salvador. Other invasions, too, have been crushed, and much of the prevailing movement has been to Villa el Salvador which has grown rapidly to be the largest of all pueblos jóvenes. The government focused many of its efforts upon this one settlement to the envy of all others: presidential visits, an express bus service from its outskirts to the city centre, speedy installation of water and electricity. The settlement was heralded to become the first *ciudad autogestionaria* (self-governing city); small, co-operatively managed industries were to create local employment.

The Pamplona invasion, together with a wave of industrial strikes, stimulated the creation of the Sistema Nacional de Apoyo a la Movilización Social (SINAMOS), a vast organization again responsible directly to the president and led by military officers, with the task of stimulating and co-ordinating all forms of community and co-operative enterprise in both urban and rural areas. ONDEPJOV was absorbed into that wing of SINAMOS dealing with the pueblos jóvenes. SINAMOS worked through the local associations of pueblo joven members, itself actively organizing elections; it increased the rate at which titles to land have been issued, though it granted titles only to those legally married. Speculation in land and house property within the pueblo joven was banned, though ineffectively. SINAMOS officials tried, although not always successfully, to prevent further invasions of land; the military government has pursued a much tougher policy in Lima that in other Peruvian cities, hoping thereby to reduce the flow of city immigrants.

Above all, SINAMOS represented a major attempt to mobilize the population from above. It sought to channel all popular demands and to weaken other modes of popular expression; it organized rallies demonstrating support for the government. Many residents in pueblos jóvenes who had successfully manipulated its bureaucratic procedures to their own ends, applauded its activity; others who saw SINAMOS as crushing local initiative decried its presence. Hostility to SINAMOS increased over the years thus destroying its *raison d'etre*; it fell into disgrace in 1975 and many thought that it would be disbanded. There was much advocacy of new policies which would embody mobilization from below; but the ideologies did not specify what local units were to form the basis of such mobilization, nor how opinions might be articulated. However, SINAMOS continued in existence for a little longer, though appearing to an increasing extent as an agent of popular control. Direct dialogue between the military leaders and the people, both in the presidential palace and at rallies in provincial towns, was the principal form of popular representation provided in the mid-70s. In 1978 SINAMOS was finally disbanded, its functions being absorbed into existing ministries; those relating to the pueblos jóvenes were undertaken mainly by the Ministry of Housing.

Plan Túpac Amaru, the national development plan of the mid-70s, promulgated as economic conditions obliged the military government to turn to more conservative and capitalist policies, said little positive about any proposed development in the urban slums.

The peripheral pueblos jóvenes of Lima are, as a consequence of these policies, among the least unattractive shanty towns of the Third World. The housing development which has taken place is quite remarkable. Yet one should, as Collier (1976) invites us to do, also ask what policies have not been considered or implemented. In spite of the radical rhetoric of the present military regime in its first seven years, and of the interest of the Peruvian intellectuals in developments in Cuba, no massive programme of urban land reform has been seriously suggested. Laws controlling rents in the inner city and towns were long awaited and recent legislation has, in effect, protected the landlords. Little use has been made of legislation enabling the acquisition of land for public use: for example, for low-cost housing estates. The profitable activities of the private housing construction companies have not been threatened. Self-help in slum housing does not produce any national redistribution of income.

The pueblos jóvenes: an overview

Settled on very different terrains – on hillsides, river banks and wide sandy expanses occupied by different modes – by slow accretion or by invasions at different periods, some pueblos jóvenes are still in the process of formation, others have been developing for 25 years; it is not surprising that they appear diverse in their characteristics. Yet in the settlement and growth of each, similar processes have been at work; and the range of house types, from matting huts to impressive two-storey brick houses, is to be found in many pueblos jóvenes.

To the unaccustomed eye these settlements seem to sprawl without local boundaries amid the hills of San Cristóbal or El Agustino, along the Canta and Atocongo roads; others, within the urban area, are clearly bounded by residential areas of markedly contrasting character. Yet in all these areas there is a strong feeling of identity in each pueblo joven, buttressed today by its official recognition; within the larger settlements, individual wards often have a surprising degree of co-operative spirit.

In 1974, SINAMOS recognized pueblos jóvenes with an estimated total population of over one million; of these almost a third (98 of them) had fewer than 500 inhabitants, nearly a quarter (74) had between 500 and 1,000 people; thus half were quite small. 19 pueblos jóvenes had over 10,000 inhabitants. Most of these large settlements are in the Caraballyo complex, such as Comas, and in the southern area there are Pamplona and Villa el Salvador; a large number of the smaller ones are in the city's residential areas, and in Callao in particular. The large settlements (with a population over 10,000) probably account for 50 per cent of the inhabitants in pueblos jóvenes; the small settlements (under 1,000) perhaps make up 10 per cent.

The JNV, in assessing potentiality of the settlements for remodelling and title grant, created a six-fold classification. The percentage of the population embraced by each category is shown in brackets: (A) Settlements on flat land with wide streets, density of population below 80 families per hectare (50 per cent); (B) as (A) but located on hillsides with less opportunity for improvement (4 per cent); (C) as (B) but with higher densities (7 per cent); (D) Irregularly settled areas, twisting streets, no open spaces and with many temporary buildings (16 per cent); (E) as (D) but with more desirable houses (16 per cent); (F) Dangerous locations and deserving of eradication (6 per cent).

Following Stokes' distinction (1962) between 'slums of hope' and 'slums of despair' and Turner's dichotomy between bridgeheaders and consolidators, Delgado (1969) based his own classification upon the basic division between inner-city slum (*tugurio*) and squatter settlement (barriada). The latter he classified with three variables: high versus low density of settlement; inner city versus peripheral; incipient versus advanced consolidation. No attempt has, however, been made to estimate the population in each of these categories.

Uzzell's intensive study (1972) of 4 pueblos jóvenes shows graphically how each has a distinctive character. Each attracted slightly different types of settlers and presented them with dissimilar opportunities. Through the choices made by these settlers, constrained both by the opportunities available and by their previous decisions, a different world emerged in each pueblo joven: different occupational structure, contrasting patterns of social networks. These were in turn reflected in a general ambience of hope and progress, or of apathy. Yet, as we shall see later, the individual settlement contains persons of widely different social characteristics and these are ignored in bestowing on the totality a generalized personality.

After emphasizing the differences between pueblos jóvenes it may seem contradictory to try to present a general overview of them in statistical terms. A wealth of material exists, from small surveys of individual settlements; these present very varied images of the pueblo joven, to some extent, one suspects, because of the different character of the settlements, but also because of varieties in sampling techniques, inadequate recording of responses and so on. A sample survey of marginality in the whole of Lima was carried out in the late 1960s by staff of DESCO and this provides most of the data (figures as in original) cited below (Gianella 1970). One of its prime advantages is that it contrasts the pueblo joven with other types of residential areas in the city: the upper-class residential areas, urbanization and housing projects, and *convencional* areas (this last category embracing the residential areas of the rest of the urban poor); it is with the last mentioned that the characteristics of the pueblos jóvenes might most usefully be compared.

It is in their overall physical appearance that the pueblos jóvenes contrast so markedly with the poorer residential quarters of the city. Many of the former are well laid out, but only one-fifth of the houses abut onto a paved street (compared with 88 per cent in convencional areas). The other qualities of the houses are summarized in the tables opposite.

Such figures reflect, of course, the recent establishment of many settlements; but those people who have managed to build a decent house may well lack essential services, possibly because the terrain raises technical problems, or because the settlement is not accorded sufficient importance to attract government aid, or because its people have been inactive in pressing for improvements.

	Pueblos jóvenes	Convencional
Type of house:		
independent	71%	41%
flats	0%	25%
single rooms	28%	32%
Construction:		
brick or cement	26%	62%
mud or wood	38%	30%
temporary materials (mats, waste-wood etc.)	36%	8%
Services:		
kitchen area in house	56%	77%
bathroom in house	37%*	84%
tap water within house	19%	79%
communal stand-pipe	31%	16%
tanker lorry supply	40%†	1%
electricity in house	47%	93%
Sewerage:		
public system within house	28%	83%
pit latrine	9%	1%
none	60%	15%

* Half of these are communal.
† By purchasing water in this way, the pueblo joven resident pays 25 times as much per litre as the householder in the city.

The DESCO survey gives no data on family composition. However, the detailed census of the newly formed Ciudad de Dios made by Matos Mar (1966) in the late 1950s graphically disproves allegations of family disorganization. Of the 936 families counted, 6 per cent were of a married couple without children, though in a quarter of these cases they lived with other relatives; 54 per cent were of both parents together with children, usually their own (that is, a nuclear family); in a further 14 per cent of cases there was a nuclear family living with other relatives who were usually young people but in some cases were grandparents; in only 21 per cent of the cases was there just a single parent with children, and often other relatives. In nine-tenths of these cases it was a mother with her children. Finally, a very small number of persons (11 in all) lived on their own, and 27 families were quite irregularly composed (in many of these a group of brothers lived together).

A correlated pattern of family stability is provided by DESCO data on home ownership. Although the homes in the pueblo joven are smaller and more overcrowded – 2.6 rooms (3.0)‡ and 2.2 persons per room (1.6)

‡ The figures in parentheses represent those for the convencional areas.

– a greater proportion are owned: 39 per cent (23 per cent) have title and a further 40 per cent (5 per cent) occupy without payment; only 16 per cent (68 per cent) are tenants. Three-quarters of the pueblo joven owners have built their homes without any type of formal credit. The titled owners generally have houses of solid construction: 44 per cent are of brick and so on, and another 44 per cent of mud or similar material; over half the non-owners live in houses built of temporary materials. Rents in the pueblo joven – for those who pay such – form only a slightly higher proportion of income, 25 per cent, than elsewhere (22 per cent), the rents of course being much lower in this type of accommodation.

The pueblo joven population contains slightly more migrants – 60 per cent (51 per cent) – than any other residential category. It is also a young and less well-educated population as the following table demonstrates:

	Pueblos jóvenes	Convencional
Age:		
0–14 years	52%	38%
15–34	30%	36%
35–49	12%	16%
over 50	6%	10%
Adult literacy (over 12 years of age):		
illiterate	8%	2%
incomplete primary schooling	40%	10%
complete primary schooling	29%	26%
incomplete secondary schooling	19%	28%
complete secondary schooling	3%	16%
further education	1%	9%
School attendance:		
5–9 year-olds in school	65%	74%
10–14 year-olds in school	94% (92% in primary school)	96% (75% in primary school)
15–19 year-olds in school	57% (29% in primary school; 2% in post-secondary education)	68% (17% in primary school; 6% in post-secondary education)
total attending state schools	89%	64%

More of the pueblo joven population are in poorer forms of employment:

	Pueblos jóvenes	Convencional
Employment type:		
Obrero (wage employees)	48%	33%
Empleado (salaried employees)	11%	32%
Self-employed	28%	18%

	Pueblos jóvenes	*Convencional*
Occupational categories:		
Artisans	32%	27%
Street-traders	28%	18%
Service trades	13%	14%
Daily paid labourers	13%	7%
Office workers	8%	15%
Sphere of activity:		
Manufacturing	34%	31%
Commerce	24%	24%
Services	22%	31%
Construction	8%	5%

Commerce embraces a variety of activities and 92 per cent (74 per cent) of the pueblo joven traders are engaged in small-scale retailing. Similarly in the service occupations fewer pueblo joven residents are employed by government: 31 per cent (40 per cent), and more, 22 per cent (15 per cent) are engaged in transport. However, although the pueblo joven residents are in the less lucrative forms of employment, 69 per cent of them (77 per cent) are recorded as adequately employed, 28 per cent (19 per cent) as underemployed and only 3 per cent (3 per cent) as unemployed. (These last figures exclude domestic servants.)

The income profile of the pueblos jóvenes and of the other poor residential areas is as follows (again domestic servants are excluded from individual incomes):

S/.monthly	*Individual incomes %*	*Family incomes %*
1 – 249	7.6 (4.0)*	⎰ 3.4 (1.6)
250 – 499	5.0 (6.0)	⎱
500 – 999	11.7 (7.9)	4.6 (1.6)
1,000 – 1,999	24.2 (21.4)	8.8 (10.0)
2,000 – 2,999	23.1 (18.9)	21.6 (13.6)
3,000 – 4,999	21.0 (20.8)	29.1 (25.8)
5,000 – 7,499	5.2 (9.5)	19.6 (18.3)
7,500 – 9,999	1.5 (4.8)	6.8 (11.8)
10,000 – 14,999	⎰	4.1 (8.8)
15,000 – 19,999	⎨ 0.7 (4.8)	2.0 (3.6)
20,000 – 24,999	⎩	– (1.6)
25,000 +	– (1.0)	– (3.3)

The pueblo joven residents are markedly poorer: their median personal income was S/.2,215 (S/.2,780) and their median family income S/.3,840 (S/.4,790). Yet a startling feature is that their less well-educated

* The figures in parentheses in both table and text represent those for the convencional areas.

members have relatively good incomes: the mean income of the illiterate being S/.1,000 monthly (S/.480) and of the primary educated person S/.2,675 (S/.1,830). The better educated are relatively poor: the secondary-school graduate earning an average of S/.1,980 (S/.2,500), and the person with higher education only S/.3,000 (S/.6,000). The more successful school leavers move out of the pueblo joven, leaving behind those who have failed to find good employment.

A survey by Lewis on employment and income in the barriadas, conducted in 1969–70, showed that the average income of individual barriada residents was S/.1,956, about one-seventh lower than the average city wage. But this average income of the barriadas was pulled down by the greater proportion of underemployed. Lewis (1973, p. 150) concludes that: 'In sum, the economic characteristics of the *majority* of barriada residents were very similar to those of the working class in Lima. Only a minority of the barriadas' residents could be considered, in one sense or another, economically marginal.' The barriada was not, therefore, a distinct economic phenomenon, that is, a settlement in which the majority of the residents were 'marginal'.

Figures such as these tend to give an image of the average – but quite atypical – pueblo joven resident. Yet the range embraced in many of the classifications gives an indication of the diversity of the population. At one extreme is the young sierra immigrant with a primary education who manages to establish himself in the city and who moves out to the pueblo joven with his family in order to be able to build his own house (for he is still too poor to qualify for public housing); he does his best to give his children a good education. At the other extreme are those evicted precipitously from a corralón or tenement for inability to pay the rent, and who arrive in the pueblo bereft of almost all possessions, seeking rented accommodation of the poorest quality; some of these may be wives deserted by their husbands; they struggle to give their children a primary education; most of these are beset by sickness and such misfortunes. The diversity in the type of person who moves into the pueblo joven is best demonstrated by a detailed examination of a single settlement.

4. Medalla Milagrosa

Medalla Milagrosa is not typical of the pueblos jóvenes of Lima; no single settlement could possibly be that, given the range of their size and age. But this little settlement of some hundred families, nestled in a gully in the cliffs, is probably representative of those smaller pueblos lying within the city; and the experiences of the people of Medalla Milagrosa are probably not dissimilar to those of thousands of others living in the vast peripheral settlements.

The foundation of Medalla Milagrosa and its subsequent growth and development derive from its location: it is situated in a little ravine leading down to the beach, on the margins of a large and upper-middle-class residential area.

For nine months of the year the sky in Lima is almost perpetually overcast, the temperatures are low (10° C–16° C midday) and the air humid – a consequence of the Humboldt current. But from January to March the sky clears and the day temperatures rise to the 20°s. Offices close at lunch-time and hundreds spend the afternoons on the beach. The old and wealthy municipality of Miraflores has developed its shore; the deep ravine cutting through the cliffs has been landscaped, groynes facilitate the extension of the sands, and kiosks and beach amusements abound. The shore road has been extended northwards and now zigzags up the steep cliffs to San Isidro; it is planned to extend it further to Magdalena del Mar. Here a little gully leads towards the sea – a gully now occupied by the pueblo joven. A few bathing-huts were built in the early 1930s to cater for the local residents but these fell into decay and were severely damaged by the earthquake of 1940. No trace of them now exists, but the municipality retains its interest in a beach approach, thwarted in part by the pueblo. A new road has been cut through the cliff top and a rough track leads down its steep side to the small stony beach. But even this area is popular in summer. The people of Medalla Milagrosa and their rich neighbours segregate themselves on either side of the groyne; several of the former operate small kiosks and barrows selling drinks and sweetmeats.

The first settlers in Medalla Milagrosa, or Bajada de los Baños ('the way down to the bathing-place') as it was first known, arrived in the early 1930s when the surrounding area was still farmed, with estates owned by some of the wealthiest and best-known members of the Limanean oligarchy. The suburbs of Magdalena del Mar (now a lower-middle-class area) had extended seawards along the Avenida de Brazil in the 1920s. At the seaward end lay the large compound of the Larco Herrera mental hospital whilst along the cliff top were sited the baroque buildings of the orphanage. In the subsequent decades the infilling of the area between Magdalena and Miraflores proceeded rapidly as the wealthy municipality of San Isidro grew towards the sea. Today the farms are no more; the racecourse has given place to President Belaúnde's urbanization of San Felipe; the polo-ground is now a very select residential block; only the British (Anglo-Peruvian) Club remains. In the last decade, building has extended across the Avenida del Ejército, the main road paralleling the cliff top, and urbanizations of middle-class housing have been built on either side of Medalla Milagrosa; Orantia, the urbanization to its south, has been completed, but that to its north side is in the process of development. For many of the residents in these two areas the view from their windows is across the gully of Medalla Milagrosa, though so steep are its sides that most of its houses are hidden from view.

Nevertheless to the municipal authorities and to land-owners (between whom many links exist) Medalla Milagrosa is an embarrassment, disrupting plans for the development of the access to the sea and creating one of those 'festering sores' in an otherwise 'highly desirable' residential area. The residents in the adjacent urbanizations firmly believe that Medalla Milagrosa is a den of thieves, the abode of those who so frequently rob them; that it is a slum of disease and filth. None would ever stroll through it, none would have much need to. It is isolated and ostracized. But after the fruitless attempts to evict the settlers, they must now, as they live in a recognized pueblo joven, be tolerated.

Medalla Milagrosa is barely visible from the main road. As it runs southward the busy Avenida del Ejército with its buses travelling to the city centre, to Callao and to Miraflores, passes the mental hospital and the orphanage and reaches the gaunt grey four-storey convent, surmounted by a cross, which provides one landmark facing the pueblo's entrance; another is a huge billboard advertising a local soft drink. A sandy track leads seawards, but as it turns and descends only the initial houses in the settlement are visible. On either side of this track the ground rises slightly; the pobladores have tried to make this area into an attractive garden but only three or four young shrubs struggle to survive. The first stand-pipe is too far away for the manual transport of water, the water pressure too low to permit watering by hose. In contrast, in the neighbouring urbanization, the verges are planted and soaked regularly by the municipality.

As one descends into Medalla Milagrosa one first passes the kindergarten on the right, its one classroom and patio hidden behind a brick wall.

This classroom is used by the *junta* (council) for its meetings and a blackboard on the outside walls announces these – or a football match. The primary school is adjacent, entered through an ornamental iron gate. Some of its windows overlooking the street are glazed, others are barred and covered by plastic sheeting. Opposite is the Club de Madres (Mothers' Club). Of brick construction, its front wall is plastered and painted blue; its doors and shutters are unpainted; its concrete roof, however, provides a grandstand for fiestas held in this area; inside it is unfurnished and its rooms are used as a communal store for building-materials. Here, as the road descends to the left, a narrow passage leads off half-right, a flight of steps uniting it with the road midway through the settlement. The pobladores think of this area as their main square, but at the junction, the community's poorest member has built a most decrepit shelter, of mud block, packing-case sides, asbestos sheet and similar detritus.

Now, however, almost all the houses of Medalla Milagrosa are of solid construction. They lie neatly aligned along both sides of street and passage, each contiguous with its neighbour. The street-facing walls are often plastered and gaily painted. Doors and windows are a symbol of affluence; some of the former are solidly carved and varnished; some houses have glass windows in metal frames, others have only wooden shutters. Outside the better houses a cement threshold provides a bench for sitting, as well as preventing the erosion of the shallow foundations. Most houses are still single-storey, their flat roofs constructed of asbestos sheet, wood and matting; some have a concrete roof in anticipation of a further storey. Waste building-material lying on the roofs gives an untidy appearance; so too do the projecting iron rods from the corners of buildings, the heaps of sand or bricks or cement blocks which, together with rocky outcrops, make the road hazardous for driving. All these are signs of ongoing building activity, the varying styles of individual initiative involved.

One or two houses at the upper end of the street have recently had a second – and in one case a third – storey added; these houses project above the level of the surrounding land. The remainder are built into the sides of the gully; some have little or no room for outbuildings, others have a small patio for storing things, keeping fowls or hanging washing (if this last is not done on the roof). These outbuildings are usually of much poorer construction. Behind one house the slope has been terraced to make a little garden but this is unique.

At its foot, the main street – only 400 metres long – terminates in a vast flat semi-circular amphitheatre; in fact, it is a raised beach from which the track leads to the shore. No building has been permitted in this area save for the new kindergarten school. One part is crudely marked out by local youths as a football pitch; their team is known as 'the donkeys' because of the hard stony pitch on which they play.

As one walks down the street one learns little of what lies behind these varied façades. The front door usually leads directly into the main living-room. Almost all houses now have a cement rather than an earth floor. But some have little furniture apart from a few wooden chairs or benches and a simple table. Others, in contrast, have linoleum, plastic-upholstered settees; a vase of plastic flowers is on the table, a corner cabinet contains the best family china. Several homes have a television; in the poorer ones, neighbours (usually the children) are admitted to watch for a small payment. On the walls are usually large photos of parents, wedding portraits and certificates of merit gained by the schoolchildren. The room often contains a bed for some of the family must perforce sleep here. Kitchens and other bedrooms are separate. Cooking is done on gas or paraffin stoves; some homes have a refrigerator and some women have a number of electrical gadgets. The most recently arrived families often live in one room which serves all functions of cooking, eating and sleeping. These quarters are inevitably squalid and cramped and contrast markedly with the neat and clean appearance of the more established and wealthier families.

In some houses the front parlour has been converted into a shop. The shops sell a wide assortment of fresh vegetables as well as an array of tinned goods and other groceries; others sell only non-perishable goods and a few have merely a refrigerator with cold drinks. The house of one of the oldest inhabitants contains a spacious bar, its wall decorated with a mural of San Martín on horseback; though some other houses also serve as bars, this one attracts a small clientele from outside Medalla Milagrosa, albeit downwardly mobile persons and some of foreign descent. The other bars and all the shops cater exclusively for the pobladores of Medalla Milagrosa, though they use the latter mainly for small quantities of daily purchases and for goods bought on credit. A weekly shopping expedition to one of the ultra-modern supermarkets of San Isidro, or to the more distant open market of Surquillo, which serves a large pueblo joven population in this area, is a regular weekend activity for many households.

At most times of the day Medalla Milagrosa is a very quiet place. The men, and many of the women too, are away at work. Those at home are busy with their household tasks and keep their front doors closed. A few can be found chatting at the stand-pipes as they tediously fill their pails of water, to replenish the drums within their house; but the drawing of water is usually the task of the children, or of youths who go late at night when the water pressure is slightly higher. During the day one sees the children depart for and return from school, clad in their uniform grey pullovers and skirts/trousers. These children often spend leisure moments sitting outside their homes talking. Small children play in the road with home-made wheeled tops; they tease their dogs and chase the odd chicken. Some young fishermen occasionally lay out nets for mending. At weekends the youths often erect a badminton net across the entrance to the pueblo; boys play on the football pitch; the *sapo* chests are brought out for men, both young and old, to test their skill at this popular Peruvian game.

The men of Medalla Milagrosa wear 'western' dress: shirt and trousers together with a pullover or sweater on colder days and a jacket, usually well worn. A few very old women, mothers of established pobladores who have come to visit or have recently migrated to be with their children, wear the traditional peasant dress of the sierra: the wide-brimmed hat, the voluminous padded skirts. The middle-aged women of sierra origin no longer wear the striking hat, but they do retain their hair in a plait; they wear a jumper, a full skirt and, frequently, long woollen stockings. The younger women, those of costa origin, and the more emancipated, wear sweater and slacks, and cut their hair short. Spanish is spoken by all except the aged newly arrived, though many have a pronounced Quechua accent. Most of those from the southern sierra frequently speak Quechua in the home. No longer is this skill a stigma, to be hidden by those who seek acceptance in urban society. Yet while some parents seem keen that their children should grow up bilingual, others are equally content that Quechua should be a forgotten language.

The growth of Medalla Milagrosa

The earliest inhabitants of the gully were those who had been working on the surrounding farmland. With the construction of the bathing-place, Señores Flores and Laura were appointed as caretakers. Their task was to keep the area tidy, free of fly-attracting refuse, and to collect fees from those using the facilities. With the destruction of the bathing-place these men continued to be in charge of the area. Gradually others invaded the gully, usually without the consent of the existing residents. A few of these were fishermen. By the end of the 1950s almost a hundred families were living in the area; from this period several attempts were made for the eviction of the pobladores.

At the end of 1958 the pobladores were given notice to leave and many were resettled in either San Martín de Porres on the bank of the Rímac, or the new Ciudad de Dios on the southern outskirts of the city. On this occasion a reprieve was obtained by exploiting the rivalry between the municipalities of Magdalena del Mar and San Isidro for this area of coast; the latter issued the quit notice, the former claiming the land as its own revoked it. But Magdalena del Mar needed the land for an international fair and so in turn sought to evict the people. On one occasion a member of the community, a policeman, was able to contact high officials and get a few months' stay of execution. Officials, landowners, the nuns from the convent, all tried to persuade the people to move to the peripheral barriadas; visits were made to view the sites selected but when the people realized that they were being given plots far in the interior of these settlements and not near the main roads, they rejected the move. Several times people moved away and their estera houses were bulldozed; most soon returned again. A few seem to have resisted translocation altogether. Other attempts at eviction were foiled through publicity given by a local radio station; or when it was allegedly discovered that the eviction order had not been discussed in the municipal council but had been issued at the behest of a wealthy local landowner. In the eyes of the pobladores these attempts represented the combination of interests of the municipality and its wealthy supporters – the landowners and the church. In the end none of these eviction attempts was successful. Some people who left, in fear or by force, did not return; but of the present residents of Medalla Milagrosa well over half had come to Bajada de los Baños before 1960. Many of the present residents, and among them many of the Huancarinos, first came to the settlement around 1960, which suggests that a positive attempt was being made to recruit new-comers and so resist eviction. One of the consequences of the repeated moves against the settlement was the formal creation of an 'Asociación de Pobladores' in 1960 when the name Medalla Milagrosa was adopted, being that of the local parish. For though the nuns from the convent had, in fact, tried to persuade the people to move, they had been active in relieving poverty, making gifts of food and clothing to the most needy; the church had, in addition, sent its social workers into the area.

The Law of 1961 gave official recognition to the community; it was eventually classed as a settlement due for eradication; its layout did not make remodelling feasible and the site was deemed to be in considerable danger of earthquake damage.

Nevertheless the national housing corporation did make a survey of the settlement and an engineer, related to President Belaúnde, began to make plans to improve it. These came to naught, however, being halted, it is alleged, on the order of a wealthy local landowner, *alcalde* (mayor) of Lima (her palatial house, six blocks away, is now the Embassy of the USSR).

The decade of the 1960s, however, did see rapid developments within Medalla Milagrosa. The persistence of the settlement attracted a few more immigrants so that all the available land was soon occupied. Latecomers have been accepted only as tenants or lodgers in existing houses. The more permissive attitude of the government was exploited, as politicians began to vie for the support of the barriada population. Settlements declared themselves 'Belaundista' and the support of influential politicians and officials was sought in obtaining services. On occasions the wife of the president visited Medalla Milagrosa. More social workers were relocated to the barriadas. A dignitary in Magdalena del Mar spoke to the Lions Club and won financial support towards the building of the Club de Madres.

Development also came to Medalla Milagrosa in a more obnoxious form. A construction firm was given permission to erect a stone-crushing machine right at the end of the main street. For eight years the noise was deafening and dust invaded every corner of the houses; it increased the incidence of lung diseases and made it impossible to hang out washing during the day. Blasting was likely to shatter glass window-panes. The material produced was used in building the new urbanizations of the area. Medalla Milagrosa profited only in the employment of a very few of its members. A promise of a big lump sum and monthly payment for the development of the community seems not to have materialized. A further cost was the loss of one child, killed by a construction lorry.

At this distance in time it is difficult to gauge the various factors at work: first, pressure by the people of Medalla Milagrosa on various authorities and through their influential contacts; second, the initiative of the latter in promoting development; and third, the measures designed to facilitate the work of the stone-crushing plant or to compensate for the hardship it caused. But within the space of a few years the central street of the pueblo was, in some measure, levelled to allow cars to use it; water was piped into the settlement, four stand-pipes being built (no house as yet has its own piped supply); electricity was brought, first to a television room at the entrance of the pueblo and later to each house, the supply being metered both at entry to the pueblo and in each home. A simple sewerage system was constructed, the waste being washed by used household water to an effluence in the cliffs. The primary school, kindergarten and Club de Madres were all built, in each case the pobladores providing much communal labour whilst outside benefactors, both state and private, provided the materials of construction.

The 'Asociación de Pobladores' of Medalla Milagrosa, founded in 1961, continued as the governing council of the barriada throughout the decade. At its inception, its president was Señor Laura, one of the earliest settlers in the gully. (Another who had preceded him had left Medalla Milagrosa for Breña, a lower-middle-class suburb nearer the city centre.) Laura was succeeded by Señor Tuestas, a relatively recent arrival but one of the better-educated men in the community; he worked in a university library and ranked as an empleado. The main tasks of the junta were to regulate entry to the community by collection of an entrance fee, which in the early years had consisted merely of drinks, but rose with the shortage of land to fees of S/.1000 or more. Their duties were also to collect a monthly fee of S/.10 from each head of household as a contribution towards community expenses; to organize communal projects; and to receive the necessary payments from each home to meet the communal bills for electricity and water.

In 1973 the association was reconstituted to meet the requirement established by SINAMOS for all pueblos jóvenes; Medalla Milagrosa was divided, rather arbitrarily, into four wards, each with its own elected committee of officers. These then elected and constituted the central committee of the community. The tasks of the latter remained largely as before. Minutes of all formal meetings were sent to SINAMOS and it was through this organization that all requests for further services were to be directed. However, few requests seem to have been made and SINAMOS officials were much more preoccupied with the larger settlements; Medalla Milagrosa has been neglected.

Origins of the pobladores

The settlers in Medalla Milagrosa have come from almost all parts of Peru; only the small departments in the extreme north and south of the country and those of the low selva are not represented. Nevertheless a third of them came from Apurímac Department and a fifth from the neighbouring Ayacucho Department; in all, two-thirds came from the mancha india. In contrast, only a sixth came from Lima department or were born in Lima city itself. Thus the sierra migrants strongly predominate. The same range of origins is seen in the earlier settlers, though in recent years the majority of immigrants have been from mancha india. Such data give an impression of great ethnic heterogeneity in the community – and this there certainly is. However, it masks the fact that every settler has been introduced to the community by a relative or close friend and that each newcomer certainly does not come as a stranger. Furthermore, of those pobladores who come from Apurimac, most are in fact from a single small village, Huancaray. A brief description of this village will help to illustrate the background, not only of its own emigrants, but that of many other sierra migrants to Medalla Milagrosa and other pueblos jóvenes.

Huancaray district now has under 5,000 people, its population falling in recent decades. It lies 30 kilometres south-west of Andahuaylas, the provincial capital with a population of just over 3,000; this is six hours' walking distance from Huancaray. The village may also be reached by road, 30 kilometres along the main sierra highway and then 30 kilometres by a very poor road. It is a mountainous area with farmland lying between 2,250 and 3,600 metres; the lower land is irrigated, the higher land is pasture.

Huancaray village itself has only 330 people, a few of these being wage employees, but the great majority independent workers, artisans, small traders and farmers. The rest of the district's population lives in a large number of small and widely scattered hamlets, many of which cannot be reached by car or lorry. Most families farm their own small plots of land, only a tenth of adult men being wage labourers in building and construction, or employees on the few larger farms.

Life in Huancaray is simple. Only a tenth of the homes have electric light, the rest use paraffin; almost all use wood for cooking. Many of the houses in Huancaray village itself have piped water and others obtain their supply from stand-pipes; but in the outlying hamlets water is drawn from the river or from wells. In the district only a tenth of the homes have a radio, a fifth a sewing-machine.

Several state and community primary schools now exist in the district; it has, too, a small secondary school (these are relatively recent; few educational facilities existed when the emigrants now living in Medalla Milagrosa left their village). Huancaray village has a church with a resident priest; some of the hamlets have a small church which the priest visits only annually, at the time of their patronal festival.

Shortage of land does not seem to be a problem in Huancaray, but opportunity to develop is. The district has one of the highest emigration rates in the province. Thus while the proportion of absentees from the entire province of Andahuaylas is 10 per cent the proportion of those remaining in the Huancaray district itself is almost 50 per cent. From some of the near-by villages a majority of emigrants have gone to Lima but from Huancaray almost half have travelled to the Chanchamayo valley, an area of new agricultural development in the selva, east of Tarma, whilst only a third went to the capital; one-tenth emigrated to Andahuaylas itself and to Cuzco. Huancarinos in Medalla Milagrosa say that it is possible to earn good money quickly in Chanchamayo as a plantation labourer; education is not a requirement and one may return frequently to care for one's land. Migration to Lima on the other hand is for the schooled or partially schooled, for they alone will have a sufficiently good chance to get established in the city; but such a move, once made, is more permanent.

A census of the mid-1960s recorded nearly 800 Huancarinos as living in Lima; a figure which is certainly much higher now with recent immigration from the village and births in the city. Of these, some 150 live in Medalla Milagrosa, earning the settlement the epithet 'little Huancaray'. Coming from such a homeland it is hardly surprising that few of these migrants in Lima have become prosperous. One of the leading figures is a motor mechanic with two small workshops in Miraflores; another owns a taxi. A Huancaray association was formed in Lima in 1932 and remains active, both in promoting welfare at home – contributing towards new schools and the like – and in helping members in the city.

The earliest settlers in Medalla Milagrosa did not come directly to Lima from their villages of origin; most arrived by stages, working first in provincial towns or on plantations nearer home. A typical pattern is that followed by one of the older residents of the settlement. He left his sierra village at the age of 15 years to work on a coastal plantation where he had a distant relative. After a few years he returned to his village but was conscripted into the army. Demobilized in Lima, he found work in the city, again with the help of relatives. Whilst in the army he travelled widely in Peru. Among the more recent arrivals, however, a pattern of chain migration of persons leaving the village directly for the capital has been much more significant.

We must distinguish here between the migration patterns of men and women. The latter find ready employment in domestic service: almost nine-tenths of those so employed in Lima are women. Middle-class families all aspire to having a full-time maid; even one or two homes in Medalla Milagrosa have a small girl working in this capacity. Over a third of these domestics are under 20 years of age for most lose their jobs if they marry or have children. A tenth, as recorded in one survey, were under 10 years of age when they arrived in Lima, a further three-tenths were between 10 and 14 years of age. The domestics tend to come from poor sierra homes; often, middle-class Lima families on tour of duty or on holiday will pick up a small girl in a little village, promising to care for her. Thus among the women of Medalla Milagrosa one encounters those who, as orphans or from broken homes, were so brought to Lima as an act of charity. Others were sent by their parents to stay with an aunt who quickly placed them in employment. These girls married youths whom they met in the course of their work or in the near-by streets: gardeners, street-traders, building workers. Usually the couple were not from the same village.

The men come to Lima at a slightly later age, in their late teens when they can perform manual labour. Some, as seen above, marry girls whom they meet in Lima. Others return to their village to marry, bringing their young wife to the capital as soon as they feel themselves sufficiently established. Almost without exception, the men, too, lodge with close relatives on arrival in Lima, and through them find work.

The earliest settlers of Medalla Milagrosa were, as we have seen, working on the adjacent farmland. But almost without exception, the later arrivals moved in from corralones within a mile or two of the gully.

Some had lived in one such site for a number of years, others seem to have moved rather frequently. All paid rent for such accommodation; sums from S/.100 up to S/.500 a month were mentioned. Some say that they moved to Medalla Milagrosa because the corralón rents were too high; others were evicted as the land was required by its owner for building. As the new urbanizations spread seawards from San Isidro many corralones were destroyed.

Many of the settlers must have *known* of Medalla Milagrosa well before their own entry to the community. Nevertheless all those who sought admission already had a good contact within the settlement, usually a close relative. The merits of each applicant were carefully considered by the existing pobladores before he was allocated land in return for a fee which rose steadily during the 1960s. It is difficult to establish whether many applications were rejected; some Huancaray families were initially refused entry but one of them 'invaded' the land, setting up an estera hut, and resisted ostracism by the community until acceptance was finally achieved. The reasons for this refusal are not now apparent; this was not the first Huancaray settler in Medalla Milagrosa. Perhaps some feared dominance by immigrants from a single village; possibly it was felt that the settlement was large enough and that rapid expansion might attract the attention of the municipal authorities who would redouble their efforts to evict the people.

The original houses of all the families were of estera, supplemented by waste-wood, asbestos sheeting and the like. In the early 1960s one man, an empleado from the northern sierra, began to build a mud-block house; stories relate that he constructed this behind his estera walls so that the authorities would not notice. For here, as elsewhere in the world, it is seen to be legitimate to destroy a home whilst it is being illegally built; once it is finished, destruction is a much more emotive action. The initiative of this Medalla Milagrosa citizen was criticized at the time by his neighbours, some perhaps fearing official reprisals. The first man to build with cement blocks was similarly criticized; some said that he wanted to live like the 'whites'. However, when the housing commission took its census in 1962, whilst half the houses in the gully were still of estera and a further sixth were of wood materials, a sixth were of mud block and a tenth had been constructed of burned brick. Most, however, still had estera roofs and all had beaten earth floors. Today, as we have seen, most of the houses are of solid construction.

The building of the houses over the past decade-and-a-half has been the work of individual families. As savings accumulate, the materials are purchased. Some of the pobladores belong to a rotating savings club at their place of work: each member pays in an identical sum each week and receives in turn the total collection. Building-materials are often obtained cheaply as members of the community hear of the disposal of surplus stocks at building sites. Many of the men of Medalla Milagrosa are builders by trade and are well able to construct their own homes; a little help from male friends and neighbours is sought for certain heavy tasks; wives and children can be useful in carrying water and so on. Similarly outside help is sought for some more complicated operations, such as erecting the reinforced pillars at the corners of the house. In general, however, there seems to have been little communal effort in building; nor have any but the richer families employed others to build their house. By far the most arduous task encountered by most families has been the digging back into the sides of the gully to make enough level ground for a house, excavating the boulders and subsequently removing the material.

Many of the resultant houses are quite spacious; nearly half have four or more rooms, though a fifth have only one room and a further fifth only two rooms. The average occupancy per room is a little over two persons; but in nearly a third of the homes there are more than three persons per room. Almost all of the houses are owner-occupied. Regulations governing pueblos jóvenes attempt to prevent the speculation in land by making it illegal to own a house or land in more than one settlement; the community itself is usually able to prevent multiple-plot-holding within its own area. A very few houses in Medalla Milagrosa are at present unoccupied; in each such case the original owner has moved elsewhere, either to another pueblo joven or to an urbanization. In most of these cases the owner is not anxious to sell his property, claiming that his children will soon need the house; in one case a sale has been sought, at an asking price of S/.80,000. Some owners have let part of their house to lodgers or tenants; it is these latter who, being in cramped quarters, argue that they should be allowed to use vacant houses, in effect to squat; this has been resisted by the community. One man has let the unfurnished top floor of his house to tenants for a sum equivalent to a quarter of the minimum wage, pending the completion of the building and its occupancy by his growing family. In several homes live one or more married children of the owner, the young couple being unable to acquire land in Medalla Milagrosa, as there is no more available, or being unable to afford either costly rented accommodation or mortgage payments on a purchased house.

The population of Medalla Milagrosa is now highly stable. Of those who resisted the eviction attempts of 1958–60, and who subsequently built their own homes of solid material, not more than 5 per cent have left the community. Many more talk of leaving but are either unable to contemplate saving enough money, or, if they do begin to accumulate capital, find that a sudden illness or similar disaster erodes their savings. One woman saved enough to move to a new urban estate, but then rejected the opportunity offered to her because the house could not be used as a shop. The population of Medalla Milagrosa is young: even in the early 1970s well under 10 per cent were over 50 years of age. The older children in most families are now reaching marriageable age; and whilst some young couples move away, there are as many who continue to live with their parents, helping them to add an extra room or two to the house. The few young immigrants who have entered the community in the past decade are all tenants or lodgers.

One notable feature is the absence of recent migrants from rural sierra areas who come to Lima and stay initially with their close relatives. One would have expected, for instance, that the established Huancaray families would be welcoming their young nephews and nieces, helping them to find work and accommodation as they themselves were helped by their elder kin, but this is not so. A possible reason is the decline in the amount of casual work available locally, with most of the vacant land now built on, and most affluent houses having a regular gardener (though many have in their windows the sign 'maid wanted'). With their own adolescent children finding it so difficult to get employment, parents are unlikely to welcome the responsibility for more youngsters of a similar age. In this, and in other ways to be discussed later, their lives are increasingly centred upon their own nuclear families.

Work

Most of the pobladores of Medalla Milagrosa work in the adjacent suburbs, either in building or in service occupations. Their choice of Medalla Milagrosa as a permanent home and their reluctance, in the period of attempted evictions, to move to one of the new peripheral barriadas, probably derived from the need to live near their employment. For though the mediation of a friend or relative is usually cited as the reason for settlement in this community, it is certain that similar relationships could have been manipulated to acquire a plot in other areas.

They arrived in Lima with little education. Some of the women had never attended school; these grew up in rural areas at a period when primary schooling was not universal and when many parents felt that education was only for boys. Most of the men had had some primary schooling; few had completed the course. Of the pobladores now over 35 years of age – that is, the parental generation – only few had received any form of secondary schooling. A few men had taken up wage employment in a provincial town near their home and subsequently come to Lima to find a better job. Similarly a tailor had been trained in the provinces before moving to the capital. But the majority arrived with no formal skills and no capital. These facts apply with even greater force to the women.

Even those who came with some capital might quickly lose it; one young lady told how her brother had loaned her money to buy a lorry-load of potatoes; these she sold successfully in Lima's central market making a handsome profit but thieves then stole the suitcase with all the money and she was destitute.

Many male immigrants, arriving with little education and no savings, found their first employment in construction, as they were hired as casual labour. One man who started as such a casual labourer later gained stable employment at the polo-ground in Magdalena del Mar; after a period in the army he returned to the polo-ground and then became a gardener in one of the large near-by houses; here, another employee taught him how to drive and he acquired his own taxi, but he lost his car in an accident as he was uninsured. He later found employment in an expatriate building company as a driver with minor administrative tasks; this was a relatively good job, but in 1976, the firm went into liquidation and he was unemployed for several months. Another man who started similarly by working in a succession of building firms, graduating to larger companies, eventually found regular employment as a labourer in the mental hospital; from here he obtained factory employment and simultaneously took an evening job working in a university library until the illegality of such double employment led him to leave the former post.

Rather more dramatic is the tale of a boy who ran away from home at the age of nine and was adopted in a succession of homes in Lima, working occasionally in restaurants; independent again, he returned to the provinces working in the mines, in a bakery, and in the army where he learned to drive. In a brief spell in his natal village he made an unsuccessful marriage; his young wife eloped with a teacher. So he returned to Lima and became an *ambulante* (a street-trader). A recent survey has shown that a fifth of the city's trade is handled by these ambulantes. He sold fruit, then ice-cream, then cooked food, gradually accumulating his capital so that he came to own the largest shop in Medalla Milagrosa. Some of the pobladores have been even more adventurous in their search for work; one travelled to Venezuela but returned after a few months because migrants such as he could only find temporary employment, employers thus evading the payment of social-security contributions. Another had spent some time in the United States but was unable to find work.

Of the male household heads in Medalla Milagrosa approximately two-thirds are wage earners but of these only one-eighth are empleados rather than obreros (the distinction being between skilled and unskilled worker rather than between white- and blue-collared employment). Of the obreros two-fifths work in the building industry, and over one-fifth in the public services, as street-sweepers, park workers and the like.

Much of the new middle-class housing in Lima has, in recent years, been constructed by very large and often multinational corporations which have developed urbanizations or estates of several hundred houses. The large building companies recruit labour at the beginning of each project and offer fairly regular employment until the completion of the estate; here one must be known to the company or to its recruiting agents. At the other end of the scale are the small private builders who obtain a contract to build a single house; these recruit their labour as and when they need it, often paying below the minimum wage for casual work and offering no stability of employment. Below these rank the independent men who have neither the skill nor the capital to build a middle-class house (and as we have seen houses in the pueblo joven are built by their owners and friends) but who do odd jobs of maintenance – painting, repairing walls – in the suburbs. This is a most insecure form of employment save for the few who can establish a regular clientele. At the bottom of the scale in Medalla Milagrosa is an elderly man, formerly a mason but who should now be classified in all probability as chronically unemployable, who trundles a wheelbarrow from one building site to another, collecting empty cement bags, crates and the like; a firm in Callao buys the cement bags for S/.2 per kilo. As men become older the better-paid jobs with the big companies are closed to them and they become increasingly reliant upon the small entrepreneurs or upon their own contacts; but work with the big firms, though paying relatively well, does not enable their employees to build up that clientele which would allow them to retire to prosperous self-employment.

Unskilled labour in the public services, in contrast, is stable though not well paid; most of those from Medalla Milagrosa enjoy only the national minimum wage. And for those at this level of remuneration, social-security benefits are minimal. Such jobs seem usually to have been acquired through contacts who have introduced a friend to the foreman when a vacancy occurred. The hours of work do not tend to be onerous and a poblador may be able to work in the municipal park in the morning and as an independent gardener in the afternoon. The independent gardeners are, after the building labourers, the largest single category of worker in Medalla Milagrosa; more then ten men are so employed. The modest houses of the neighbouring affluent suburbs have relatively small but very well-kept gardens; yet their owners seem incapable of tending them, of mowing a pocket-handkerchief-sized lawn or weeding a flower bed. The gardener owns a tricycle and cart in which he carries his hand lawn-mower, shears and basic tools; he spends a few hours or half a day at each house, visiting some twice weekly. Whilst mowing, weeding and pruning, he looks after the sprinkler, for without constant watering, little would grow. Working thus for two shifts a day – from 7a.m. until 1p.m.

and 1p.m. until 6p.m. – a gardener with a regular clientele could earn almost twice the minimum wage. One of the pobladores in Medalla Milagrosa started work as a factory labourer where he worked in the gardens, then under the patronage of an established private gardener, worked with him at weekends, and when the factory closed took up full-time gardening himself.

Such an occupation gives little opportunity for advancement; from an apprenticeship status one progresses to independence with a full set of tools; but beyond this one cannot move. Ideally one might set up a contract service, hiring one's own labourers but it would be difficult to offer a superior service for a lower price. One of the Medalla Milagrosa gardeners discussed the possibility of a formal union of gardeners from which one advantage could be to render them eligible for social security; but this too would be difficult to achieve. The gardeners are many and come from no single rural area. Gardening is seen as a very pleasant form of work and one poblador said that he would not go back to building even though he might earn more. One of its advantages is the contact it gives with the professional middle classes; one employer is a doctor and can advise on treatment for a sick child; another is a lawyer who will help with forms; while another might find employment for one's child. These services need not be confined to the employee's own family; in promoting something which benefits the entire community, one's status in it is thereby enhanced.

Very few people in Medalla Milagrosa work in factories; not more than five men and women (and one husband and wife both work in the same factory). Much of Lima's industry lies between the city centre and Callao, and the pueblos jóvenes of the latter are obviously better located for the workers; other factories lie to the north and east of the city, much closer to the peripheral barriadas of these parts. Most of the remaining pobladores are therefore, like the gardeners, self-employed. The community has a tailor and a shoemaker, both of whom work for small firms in Miraflores. With a recent tightening-up of labour legislation – establishments with more than five employees being subject to the labour code – most small workshops manufacturing clothes or shoes for a quality market which sell in boutiques in the fashionable shopping centres have dispersed their erstwhile workers to their homes and resorted to 'putting-out' practices; that is, the firm supplies the materials and buys the finished product. The workers realize that the firm pays them only a fraction of what the goods finally sell for in the shops – and this is galling; yet they are able to save some of the material used to make goods on their own account, and their income is not reduced by social-security payments; but to do so, they gamble with their health. The tailor has a young man sent to him for training by his own master in Cuzco. But the craftsmen in Medalla Milagrosa have not, as yet, been able to build much more prosperous businesses. One handicap is the location of their homes; a rich clientele does not want to come to the shanty towns seeking out the craftsmen. The tailor aspires to move to one of the new lower-middle-class urbanizations between Medalla Milagrosa and Callao where he feels that he will be able to expand his business.

The shopkeepers in Medalla Milagrosa have already been mentioned; in only two cases is the shop the main occupation of the male household head; in all others it is minded by the wife. These shops serve, almost exclusively, the people of Medalla Milagrosa, usually selling at higher prices than the suburban supermarkets (some of which are now government-owned and sell, to their middle-class customers, basic food-stuffs at controlled prices often well below those obtaining in the open market), but willing to sell small quantities on credit. Apart from those masons who are, very occasionally, hired by their neighbours to build a house, the women who do a little sewing for other pobladores, and the few landlords, these traders are the only persons whose livelihood derives from the community itself, and they alone are solely dependent upon it.

A few other occupations might be cited. One resident is a retired policeman; one, rather strangely, is a market-gardener. He has a plot of land far away in Monterrico where he grows strawberries and keeps some livestock, selling his produce in the main Parada market. But he is threatened by the continuing encroachment on his land by building development. One of the gardeners has a barrow from which, each evening, he sells *anticuchos* (sweetmeats) at a near-by busy crossroad; his wife helps to prepare the food during the day. Two men are taxi-drivers; to own and drive one's taxi is a lucrative and much-sought-after occupation, but as the example cited above indicates, the risks are high. Vehicles are underinsured and an accident can destroy one's capital at a blow. It needs a cautious and lucky man to reach the ideal of owning a fleet of cars, employing his own drivers.

The work undertaken by the women is rather less varied. As we have seen, most of those who came to Lima at an early age worked as domestic servants. Here their experiences were varied (Smith 1971, 1973, 1975; Rutte 1973). Some existed almost in a condition of slavery, being required to work far into the night, rarely being allowed out, given little clothing and fed meals very inferior to those enjoyed by the family. Many absconded from one employment, but failed to find anything much better. Legal codes regulating the employment of domestics are widely disregarded, especially by the lower-middle classes; one such require-ment is that girls be given time off to attend school, yet many notices displayed in suburban windows indicate that a girl expecting this benefit will not be employed. Other young women were much more fortunate:

some found very generous if not wealthy employers; cases were recorded in which the employer sought to retain the services of the domestic even after marriage, offering to give accommodation to the husband and to a young child, but young couples preferred the privacy of their own home and the fear that a child might break something valuable would have created too much tension. Others again worked in rich homes, being both well paid and well treated, and themselves enjoying a style of life far above that usual among the poor. One of the wives in Medalla Milagrosa worked for a well-known artist; it is perhaps not a coincidence that she is a very nicely dressed modern young woman, that she smokes and drinks in public (to the consternation of some of the sierra women) and lives in one of the best-furnished houses (but her elder sister, also resident in Medalla Milagrosa, dresses and keeps a home in the fashion of most other sierra migrants.

Most domestics are expected to 'live in' and marriage and/or child-bearing terminates this career. A few opportunities exist for full-time domestic employment of those living in their own homes, but such work is incompatible with a wife's household duties. Some Medalla Milagrosa women do part-time domestic work, working either mornings or after-noons, or a few days each week. In such cases they are expected to do house-cleaning or the laundry. Again, a few take in laundry. Others work as domestics in the near-by institutions: the convent, orphanage and mental hospital; one woman does the mid-morning cooking for the kindergarten. Many women say that they would welcome an opportunity for part-time work but that opportunities do not seem to exist; others claim that they cannot expect neighbours to mind their children for them and so cannot be absent from home.

Other occupations open to these women are the selling of cooked food to workers at building sites and the sale of drinks on the beach during the summer months. In each case a licence must be obtained, either from the building firm or from the municipality as is appropriate, and this usually demands influence and the services of a friend to type the *solicitud* (an application on a special legal paper and couched in formal jargon).

The women in full-time employment tend to be the better educated and more skilled; they are employed in the local institutions and in two cases, in factories. Three women are well-qualified dressmakers and these work, like the male craftsmen described above, for suburban boutiques. They too feel that Medalla Milagrosa is not a good place from which to operate, though two of them do in fact live in the first houses in the community next to the school and their patrons can park their cars outside their homes and need venture no further into the settlement.

The younger generation, the children of the immigrants to Medalla Milagrosa, who are now entering the labour market do so on terms very different from those of their parents. They are, for instance, much better educated. In each adolescent age group there are as many with secondary schooling as with primary education. Their parents, successfully established in the city, have a greater and more valuable range of contacts. But these youths have little or no capital; they are the elder children of quite large families who are reluctant to be a continuing drain on their family's resources. Most of them aspire to some form of professional training and a career, and this, too, is the wish of their parents.

Ten youths, at the time of the study in 1977, had successfully entered state universities, though only two – one a girl studying engineering – were full-time students. The others attended evening classes and did odd jobs during the day. Thus they worked as builders' mates or painters, often being paid a half or less of the minimum wage. Others worked as porters in the near-by San Isidro market. The low income was not a prime consideration; they were anxious to earn to contribute to the household budget, but wanted flexibility so that they could pursue their studies. Others pursued similar employment whilst attempting to enter university; far more were trying than would ultimately succeed. Some studied at private colleges which gave preparation for the entrance examinations (often of such a quality as to be deemed a racket); others studied privately. Two of the older university students in Medalla Milagrosa talked of organizing a small class for the youths of the community, and though nothing came of this, both were actively helping their friends. Others had set their sights lower and had acquired professional training: one son had been to a naval training college, another was a medical auxiliary in the mental hospital, another a trained teacher. The outstanding success story of the community is that of a young woman (daughter of the poor mason who collected cement bags and of his previous wife now living near-by in Medalla Milagrosa and married to another builder); she passed through university where she was active in student politics, studied to become a teacher, married and emigrated to Guatemala where she became a popular singer.

For those who, through lassitude or their parents' lack of interest in education, fail to begin or to complete their secondary schooling, the initial choice of work is in the same range: odd building jobs, market porterage and the like. Some gardeners and domestics have introduced their children to their own occupations, though it is usually difficult to find enough extra work for another pair of hands. Others, in wage employment, have been able to get their sons a place in their own work-place, in the municipal services for instance, as unskilled labourers. Some youths have obtained semi-skilled employment through the help of friends of their parents or of other residents of Medalla Milagrosa. For none has the entry into stable employment been easy or quick; a period of doing odd jobs seems inevitable, though this may be exaggerated because youths seek this form of employment during school holidays and, too, during term time inasmuch as schools operate separate morning and afternoon sessions in order to cope with the numbers of pupils seeking an education.

The examples of career patterns cited at the beginning of this section give an impression of considerable job mobility; but these examples were perhaps of men of greater initiative, in addition often entering into occupations with a greater risk of failure. For the overall picture in Medalla Milagrosa is of stability. The majority of the pobladores are still in the same occupation as when they first settled in the community. On reflection this is hardly surprising.

Those employed in the public sector as labourers have security, but their incomes are insufficient to enable them to save enough to start a business of their own; those in well-paid wage employment – for example, the man working in the university library – have little inclination to change; they are getting too old to begin another career. The gardeners have established a regular clientele but they also cannot progress further. Those in building construction have irregular employment but they continue in the same trade; their mode of work does not bring them into contact with other opportunities; their aspirations are to become prosperous small entrepreneurs; in reality they become the underpaid employees of the latter when their age reduces their chances of being hired at the big building sites. The craftsmen – tailor and shoemaker – are not likely to change their trade though they may move from employment in a small workshop to self-employment with its varying degrees of economic independence. A few occupations – taxi-owning is a good example – carry high risks and a consequent rapid turnover of personnel.

Most men are, however, in a rut from which they cannot escape; realistically they expect to complete their working lives in their present occupations, and to transfer their hopes for mobility to their children. And so it is among the youths that one finds a high degree of movement: firstly as they take odd jobs whilst studying or waiting for professional training, and secondly as they leave one apparently safe career path for another which seems to promise ultimately greater rewards. In consequence there is little open unemployment in Medalla Milagrosa, though this term needs to be clearly defined. Men are not out of work because a large employer has suddenly laid off scores or hundreds of its employees; the casual labour market is sufficiently large to enable most – especially the ageing masons and the youths newly seeking jobs – to find work for much of the time; though such men do spend many days fruitlessly looking for work. With the economic recession of the late 1970s, finding jobs became increasingly difficult and many more men were unemployed for long periods. Some gardeners do not have regular contracts for all periods of the week. Many women say that they would like to work if opportunities compatible with their duties as housewives were to exist. In these senses there is underemployment in Medalla Milagrosa.

In describing how they obtained their present and previous jobs, the men and women of Medalla Milagrosa invariably acknowledge the help given by patrons. Aunts find domestic employment for their nieces in homes known to them; men in a supervisory post allocate vacant jobs to their friends and relatives; a new trade is learned from a friend or neighbour; one's immediate boss procures one's advancement into a better position in the firm. There is little mention of queuing at the gates of factory or building-site hoping to be hired, nor of applying to a labour exchange, though these do exist in Lima. Advancement follows the same pattern: the exploitation of relationships with social equals, relatives and neighbours, and with one's employers in the higher social classes.

The factory workers in Medalla Milagrosa are trade union members, and one woman so employed is a minor official in her union. But the majority belong to no such association. Building workers are notoriously poorly organized; the unions of the unskilled public employees are weak. Many who are eligible for union membership evade it; one man explained how he used the ambiguity of his position as a driver in a building construction company to join neither the drivers' nor the builders' union; he saw himself as the bosses' man, the one on whom the everyday running of the firm really depended. For the gardeners, an association existed only as an idea.

In considering both attitudes and incomes we must remember that the household, rather than the individual, is the effective unit. Several men have two jobs: the municipal labourer who does private gardening in the afternoons, the gardener who sells anticuchos in the evenings, and the municipal labourer who owns the pueblo's premier bar. The nature of the work of husband and wife, as of parents and children, may differ; husband is a wage-earning obrero, wife a part-time domestic servant.

The estimation of individual incomes in a community such as Medalla Milagrosa is difficult; the exact calculation of gross family incomes, and the modification of these totals in the light of the size of the household or the relative independence of married children, is almost impossible. Yet the great differences of wealth which exist within the community are only too apparent. At one extreme is the collector of cement bags, making but a few *soles* each day and yet supporting a wife and her children by him; or the rather wayward taxi-driver whose young wife has already borne him eight children, at annual intervals. At the other end of the scale are a couple, each of whom is in good wage employment, whose joint earnings – equal to six minimum wages – are nearly approximate to those of a junior university lecturer. A considerable range seems to have existed since the early days of Medalla Milagrosa. In the survey conducted by the housing corporation in 1962, about a sixth of the households had little or no visible income; these were headed by widows and so on; a tenth earned between S/.100 and S/.200 weekly. But a sixth received over S/.400 weekly, the top earner being a carpenter with S/.600. Very crudely the top sixth of the population earned four times as much as the bottom sixth (excluding those not earning at all). Figures for a decade later give a similar picture: in a sixth of the households the income per head was below S/.400 monthly, whilst in a fifth it exceeded S/.1,000. Recalculating these figures it would seem that a quarter of the families received less than S/.3,000 monthly which was approximately the income of one man with a minimum wage, whilst another quarter had an income of over S/.6,000.

These differences are reflected, of course, in life-styles, though not always in the most obvious manner. Some families put more of their money into their houses and furnishings, others into the private education of their children; the former families are often from the costa and one suspects them of being downwardly mobile; the latter are most often sierra families of humble rural origin. In some families a smaller proportion of the husband's earnings reaches the household economy, the remainder being spent on drink and his personal luxuries. Such factors tend in some cases to bring a family closer to the mean (the well-paid but extravagant husband), in others to propel it further away (the extravagant poor or the sober ascetic rich). Income statisticians ignore these glosses in their generalizations; in the small community they have a pronounced effect on the perceptions of social status.

Family life

As one visits the homes in Medalla Milagrosa the immediate impression is of the prevalence of a stable family life; the image of social disorganization portrayed in the graphic descriptions of Oscar Lewis certainly does not seem appropriate in this Peruvian shanty town. A quarter, perhaps, of the households are headed by a single spouse: usually an elderly woman either widowed or separated from her husband; though in one instance a widower maintains his several children, not wanting to remarry. One man in his thirties remains a bachelor but he seems unique; no women of similar age live without a man. Those couples legally married (*casado*) out-number those who are merely living together (*conviviente*) by two to one; some of the latter may eventually marry. The difference in legal status rarely occurs in conversation and, overtly at least, seems to make little difference to marital behaviour. Marriage is often delayed through the inability to save enough money for the expected celebrations.

As one delves more deeply into life-histories this idyllic picture is

modified. Several women have experienced one or two previous marriages which have ended by death or separation; in some cases the
husbands had died very young. Some men too have lost young wives. One
woman was married against her wishes when very young to a trading
partner of her father and this marriage ended disastrously. However,
contrary to popular belief, there seems little indication that in Medalla
Milagrosa men drift away from their marriages as they grow older, and as
they are less able to maintain their families financially.

Not all marriages are equally happy of course. While some wives speak
in glowing terms of their husbands' sober habits, others accuse their men
of spending too much on drink and other women, though cruelty to
themselves is rarely cited. In one family the wife was considering getting a
divorce because her husband, a gardener, was having an affair with a maid
in one of the houses in which he worked and rarely returned to his home.
But this too, at the time, appeared to be an isolated case. Legal divorce is
possible, though difficult to obtain, for unscrupulous lawyers may deal
less than fairly with poor and ignorant clients. By law, the ex-husband
should pay alimony though this again is difficult to enforce.

The number of children tends to be high: in Medalla Milagrosa there
are almost four children in each family. As many of the families are still
young, the number of children in completed families is often from six to
eight. Large families are not spoken of with approval; in fact, parents
complain of the costs of feeding and educating such a number. Ignorance
of contraception, its high costs, and the absence of schemes to popularize
birth-control, all contribute to general passivity towards the practice.
These children live with their parents in almost all cases. One woman,
thirty years of age, and married to her second husband who is several
years younger than herself, has two very young children by him; two older
boys of her first marriage are in the orphanage and stay with her only at
weekends. A young unmarried mother sought an adoptive home for her
child so that she could obtain full-time work; she finally decided to keep
her child with her. These are exceptional cases; one does not hear of
children separated from their parents through extreme poverty or delin-
quency. In fact some families in Medalla Milagrosa have taken in a child
as an act of charity; in one home there is a retarded youth who has left the
orphanage; others may have a young girl working as a maid.

In a few homes live aged grandmothers, though they are often
described as being on extended visits rather than as permanent residents.
Relatives of the parental generation – their siblings for instance – are
rarely encountered within the household (though many such constitute
neighbouring households). In several cases married children live in a
parental home; they tend to form a semi-independent household, occupying their own room and doing their own cooking. One exception to this

rule was a young widower who lived with his parents; his mother cared for his children along with her own younger children.

Another myth about the shanty town is the prevalence and strength of the trait of *machismo* among the men. However dominant this may be in those dominated by a Spanish cultural tradition, it seems rare among the Indian people. The sierra migrant in the pueblo joven is a quiet, reserved and very gentle man, not given to boasting or displays of exuberance. Domestic roles are, indeed, markedly segregated: few men do any cooking, drawing of water, or the more intimate tasks of child care. Yet they are active and helpful in the home. Children do not in general have an image of a warm affectionate mother and a stern authoritarian father; their relationship with each parent seems similar. Both parents seem to take equal responsibility for decisions affecting the children and the household. (Though one man claimed that he was building a house outside Medalla Milagrosa but had not told his wife; she abused him for squandering his money on women!) In the course of the research, women – who tended to be more readily available than men – spoke frankly of their husbands' careers; in the home they showed no reserve in joining in an interview of the husband, and both men and women would withdraw with equal grace, claiming the call of household duties, if the interview concerned only one spouse. This relative equality between men and women is reflected in the upbringing of the children; in almost all respects young boys and girls are treated alike and expected to perform similar household tasks. However, it is only the boys who at 9 or 10 years of age play football in the street. The education given to girls tends to fall behind that of boys, though many do attend secondary school. But only one of the ten university students in 1977 was a young woman. Parents hoped that their daughters might become secretaries or nurses though fewer aspired to a professional career for their daughters than for their sons. Only in some very poor families did parents expect their daughters to enter domestic service, with the hope of obtaining a good employer.

Inter-family ties

As we have seen already, almost every family which joined the Medalla Milagrosa settlement did so through the mediation of a close kinsman already living in the community. No family is thus a complete isolate. Kinship ties unite many of the Huancarinos; in addition several of these women have known each other from childhood having attended the same village primary school. Yet such relationships do not necessarily imply close affectionate bonds now; one informant alleged that she saw very little of her own brother who lived at the opposite end of Medalla Milagrosa.

Further links are created by godparenthood (*compadrazco*). A few leaders in Medalla Milagrosa seem to be godparents to a number of children; their duties toward the child seem slight; they will perhaps use their influence to find employment. Although between natural parents and godparents exists a bond which might be manipulated in a specific situation when help was required, there seem to be few regular manifestations of the tie. Some specifically preferred to select godparents from outside of Medalla Milagrosa. In general this institution of compadrazco does not seem to be strongly developed in Medalla Milagrosa, reflecting perhaps the apathy towards most religious observances.

Several youths in Medalla Milagrosa have found their spouses within the community. Some of these marriages seem to have been precipitated by an unplanned pregnancy. Young men and women play together at weekends at the entrance to the pueblo, and few have any other opportunity for recreation; they do not belong to youth clubs in the near-by suburbs, and visits to the cinema or dances are costly; work and study leave many with little free time. No contacts exist with young people from the surrounding affluent estates.

The quantity of such ties of kinship, godparenthood and intermarriage is impressive; for the researcher it is a puzzle to unravel as new links are continually being disclosed. An impression builds up of a tightly knit community in which 'everybody is related to everybody else'. Yet this is countered by the independence of the families of Medalla Milagrosa. Firstly, these ties unite one family with relatively few others; the subsequent links through these to the remaining families are tenuous, to be exploited only in crises and not in everyday living. Kin and neighbours gossip on their doorsteps and at the stand-pipe; men talk as they drink in the bars in the evening. There is a little but not much borrowing of utensils and food among neighbours. In some homes a grandmother or an older daughter will look after small children whilst their mother works; but women do not expect other wives to perform this task for them and it seems rare for a neighbour to act in this role. We already know that kinsmen and neighbours give little help in house construction; building is certainly not a collective activity. Some families seem fairly gregarious, being active in the life of the community; in turn others are withdrawn. In the latter, men return home each evening and become secluded in the privacy of their homes. In these families the children are usually kept within the house and are rarely seen playing in the street. In other homes, too, parents active in community affairs discourage their children from playing outside, arguing, in familiar tones, that they should not associate with rough children but should concern themselves with their studies.

The picture given here of the stable nuclear family, contrasting so vividly with the social disorganization so often assumed to exist in slum communities, must be modified by a recording of family misfortunes. For as one goes from house to house, so many of them seem to have a problem. In some, the wife, still only in her forties or fifties, is chronically ill, perhaps with arthritis or a heart complaint; one wife is almost paralysed. The men seem fitter, though one young man nearly lost his eyesight, perhaps through overstrain as he worked long hours as a tailor; he underwent a serious operation and spent many months in convalescence and recuperation, much of the time in his home village; his entire career plans had to be changed; he now works as an electrician. Another young man is an alcoholic and is capable of getting only casual work. One family has a spastic child, another a deaf child. Several children have been psychologically disturbed: one used to come home from school and shut himself in his room studying; a small boy in the kindergarten took no part in its activities but just sat by the wall. Some of these misfortunes are perhaps due to poverty and poor housing – remember that in the 1950s and early 1960s the people of Medalla Milagrosa were living in estera huts without water, electricity or sewerage. Others arise from a pressure to succeed, placed by parents on themselves or upon their children. In most cases treatment had been sought and obtained in a hospital or psychiatric clinic; but few pobladores are adequately covered by social security and so one finds discontinued treatment or the trial of one remedy after another, from doctors, herbalists and the like, in an attempt to find quick and effective relief and cure. Much of a family's hard-earned savings are quickly eroded, often dashing their hopes of being able to afford a house outside Medalla Milagrosa in an urbanization. Life seems a game of snakes and ladders, with the snakes only too frequently encountered. Statistically, some ought to succeed in reaching the final goal and leaving the community; but the opportunities for occupational success are few, the hazards – of health, legal problems, large-sized families – are many. And of those who do save, many prefer to invest in their children's education rather than in their own material comfort.

On my return visit to Medalla Milagrosa in 1977 it seemed that the community had changed but little in the two intervening years, though inflation had certainly brought greater hardship. However, the fortunes of a few families had dramatically altered. A prosperous shopkeeper had been forced by his wife's serious illness to sell his entire stock in order to pay medical bills; being in his fifties and with poor eyesight he found wage employment impossible to get. Another man had lost a good job when his building firm collapsed; he had found alternative but less remunerative employment. The effects of such misfortunes were seen not only in material poverty but also in the despair and apathy which now pervaded the families.

Extra-community links

Most of the adult pobladores of Medalla Milagrosa have at least a few relatives living elsewhere in Lima. Rarely of course are these parents, for most of those continue to live in the village of origin. Their children are also few: their families are still young and only the older children have reached the age of marriage and an independent household. Some of these, as we have seen, continue to live in Medalla Milagrosa with their parents. Others live in pueblos jóvenes elsewhere; one such son lives at Villa el Salvador, where to the envy of his parents he enjoys more services. Most of the near-by kin are thus siblings or cousins. Here one finds considerable differences in wealth as one emigrant and his children do relatively well in the city whilst another struggles in poverty. Several of the pobladores report having kin who are professional persons, living in the lower-middle-class suburbs; some say they rarely visit these relatives and are not visited by them; others claim that mutual visiting does take place. It does seem likely that the apparent squalor of Medalla Milagrosa adds to the feeling of social distance between these kinsfolk and is a deterrent to their interaction.

Increasing age, and sickness too, confines people to the settlement. Many elderly women complained that they used to get about much more, but that arthritis and similar complaints now limited their activities. The local bus service is frequent but at rush hours the vehicles are grossly overcrowded and uncomfortable.

The most significant links for the majority of people are with relatives in their home community and with members of that community living in Lima. The continuing relationship between urban migrants and their village of origin is so often described in the literature that the picture given is perhaps overdrawn. As several writers have shown, urban associations are much more frequently created by some types of community than by others. Thus in Africa one finds differences between ethnic groups (Lloyd 1967, p. 201–3); for Latin America Roberts (1974b) has contrasted the propensity of the sierra Indians of Peru to form clubs with the absence of these associations among the mestizo urban migrants in Guatemala; and in Peru it is the small rural communities, largely homogeneous in population, which form such clubs, not the provincial towns or their suburbs. Provinces and departments do in fact have their clubs but these are organizations for those who have succeeded in the city, their functions being comparable with rotary clubs, masonic lodges and the like. Again, the urban voluntary association has usually been studied by the social anthropologist, who traces in the city the people from the village or ethnic group which he previously studied; there is thus a tendency to find those people who do maintain their links with their home area and to stress the significance of these links. When, in contrast, one takes the small urban community as the unit of study one finds that many of its members have, in fact, few or no links with their birthplace.

The Huancaray club is probably one of the better organized of the district associations in Lima. It has had nearly fifty years of continuous existence; ten hamlets have their own organization within the parent association. The latter has its headquarters in its own building; this was at Santa Cruz but is now at Surquillo, much farther away from Medalla Milagrosa. Members have been active in promoting the development of the home community: a girls' primary school and a medical post were built, funds being raised in Lima by subscription and by the organization of fiestas. One Huancaray man in Medalla Milagrosa said that he received much help from his co-villagers in planning the building of his cement-block house. Another resident received a gift of S/.5,000 from the club when her young husband died, the money being donated for the education of their son.

Many other pobladores in Medalla Milagrosa belong to village clubs which are as active as that of Huancaray. Both Huancarinos and others of sierra origin vary widely in the degree of their participation in such clubs and in the closeness of the links which they maintain with their home communities. At one extreme is the orphan girl, taken from her community at a very early age to enter domestic service; she has almost no knowledge of her home and has lost contact with relatives. One such person even took her employer's name as her own surname. At the other extreme are those who still hold land in the village and who return home annually, arranging that their holiday should coincide with the planting season. Their relatives in the village maintain the farm for the remainder of the year. Others retain ownership of land, but either put it in the care of a close relative or rent it out on a more formal basis; they then visit their farm less frequently. Such continued holding of land is, with the progress of agrarian reform, becoming more difficult as the communal land of the community may be held only by those permanently resident. One woman in Medalla Milagrosa recently sold her plot and intended using the money received to improve her house. Most of those with continuing land rights talk of returning to their home village in their old age; so, too, do those who were not farmers or who have lost their land, but the opportunities for employment in the rural area remain small and one anticipates that most will end their days in Lima. Many other pobladores, not holding farmland, nevertheless return home every few years to visit relatives. Equally, there are others who do not; some women from Huancaray say that they have not been home since they first arrived in Lima, a period of twenty or more years. This they attribute to the cost and difficult nature of the journey and the problems raised by their children who are too young or too numerous either to take on the journey or to leave in the care of neighbours. But the husbands of such women have visited home, and the women interact closely with co-villagers in Lima.

Home visits are not strongly correlated with activity in the Lima club. Thus among the Huancarinos in Medalla Milagrosa are some who return regularly to their farms but who are inactive in the club. They argue that their own work in the city, their duties as office-holders in Medalla Milagrosa, and the distance of the club headquarters all deter them from a fuller participation. They nevertheless pay subscriptions and contributions when asked. Others, in contrast, are more active club members though their links with the home community are becoming weak; thus those who have not been home recently often maintain strong ties with their co-villagers in Lima; youths who have rarely visited the family home may be loyal members of its football team in Lima. The presence of a large number of Huancarinos in Medalla Milagrosa undoubtedly reinforces the links of each individual member both with the home village and with the local club. Other pobladores in Medalla Milagrosa are the sole representatives of their particular village here and are often widely separated in distance from other co-villagers; others again come from areas which have no local club. Their ties with their home area are in general weaker; though there are exceptions: one of the earliest settlers in Medalla Milagrosa is still a leading member of his village club.

It is tempting to see the shanty town as a dormitory suburb: a place where people return to sleep, their active lives being spent mainly in their place of work or in leisure activities external to the settlement. Medalla Milagrosa *is* a quiet community: for most of the day the majority of its adult residents are away at work; they return home physically tired. But they have enjoyed little social life in their place of work. Among workers on a building site a feeling of camaraderie may develop, but with such irregular work lasting friendships are not created. Gardeners and domestic servants have little opportunity to meet people other than their employers, with whom interaction is often minimal and informal, or the tradesmen who call. With the weekends occupied by overtime work, shopping and chores within the house there are few hours left for lively associational activity with relatives or co-villagers.

Most people's lives are thus centred on their homes and on their community. The home is important because of family contact and because one can relax there; sometimes there is a television, more often a radio. One's prestige in the community is measured by the style of one's house, by the success of one's children in school and in rising out of the poorer strata. And it is the opinion of the co-residents of the community that matters most – rather than that of workmates or co-villagers scattered across the city.

Community organizations

Since its formal inception in 1961 Medalla Milagrosa has had its governing council: first the 'Asociación de Pobladores', then the SINAMOS
committees. As has been mentioned earlier the first president of the
Association was Señor Laura, the earliest settler following the departure
of Señor Flores, the founder of the settlement. He was followed from
1966 to 1969 by Señor Tuestas in whose period of office many of the
services were brought to Medalla Milagrosa. On the walls of the living-
room in Tuestas' house are certificates awarded by SINAMOS, the
municipality and other such bodies congratulating him upon his efforts
for the community. Tuestas was succeeded by Señores Ortega and Inga
each of whom held office for a short period only. The roles played by
these leaders will be discussed in the next chapter.

In 1973 the government of the community was reorganized to comply
with the pattern established in SINAMOS. The settlement was divided
arbitrarily – for the divisions do not follow recognized territorial boundaries within Medalla Milagrosa – into four wards, each having its own
council or *junta*.

The central committee of Medalla Milagrosa is composed of the senior
officials from each ward committee. Under the SINAMOS rules these
ward committees are elected annually, only household heads (or plot-
holders) being allowed to vote or to stand for election. Men who are
politically active are ineligible for election; this was an apparent attempt
to make the committees representatives of the local populace and not
vehicles for party mobilization. (But as none of the pobladores of Medalla
Milagrosa were politically active in the early 1970s, this regulation has
been of no consequence.) The presently constituted ward committees
embrace a fifth of the household heads in the community. All give their
services freely, for there is no payment for services either by the community or by SINAMOS. Meetings are held, usually late in the evening, in the
kindergarten; minutes are kept only of the more formal meetings. The
committees seem to meet about once a month, although some have to
reconvene on successive days owing to the non-attendance of several
members.

The tasks of these committees have already been listed. In the early
1960s, the Association controlled entry to the community, allocating
vacant land in return for an ever-increasing fee. A monthly subscription
helped to defray expenses; this is now in abeyance. The charges for water
and electricity are collected so that a single payment is made to the
providing authority. The committees are responsible for the general
development of the community. In addition to the grant of legal title to
the land, improvements under discussion include the provision of street-

lighting, the levelling and tarring of the road, and the creation of a garden at the entrance to the community. The committees are also responsible for ensuring that the pobladores do not extend their buildings in such a manner as to infringe the rights of others or build on areas earmarked as public places. Their failure to stop the erection of a particular poblador's house will be discussed later.

The kindergarten and primary school are still seen as belonging to the community; though both are now state-controlled, the people of Medalla Milagrosa contributed substantially towards their development. The kindergarten cares for about thirty children each morning, enabling many mothers to go out to work. Most of these children are from Medalla Milagrosa, though a few come from near-by corralones. The president of the Parents' Committee is in fact not a resident of Medalla Milagrosa though he is well known to its inhabitants; he has a barrow from which he sells cooked food every morning at the entrance to the community; he has expressed a wish to hold land in Medalla Milagrosa. For nine years since its inception – that is, until the end of 1975 – the kindergarten was managed by a woman who, though now a resident of Magdalena del Mar, had lived for a short period with an aunt in Medalla Milagrosa; she was helped by a young assistant and a nutritionist, both middle-class persons employed by the municipality. A mid-morning meal was prepared for the children by one of the women of Medalla Milagrosa. At Christmas-time a group of wealthy residents from Magdalena del Mar comes, on a Saturday morning, to distribute toys to each child in the school and baskets of food to those mothers lucky in the raffle; the ceremony – the only occasion when these visitors are seen at the school – ends with speeches of gratitude and much condescension on the part of the visitors.

The primary school has over one hundred pupils in its five classes; the two senior classes are small and share a single classroom. Many of its pupils, too, come from outside Medalla Milagrosa. The school would appear to be of an average standard. Many parents in Medalla Milagrosa seem satisfied with it; but an equal number are highly critical, saying that the teaching is poor, the teachers themselves delinquent and uninterested in their pupils. These latter parents either send their children to private schools outside Medalla Milagrosa or they obtain admission to other state schools, though they live outside their legal catchment area. The Medalla Milagrosa primary school has children who have started their schooling late, so that adolescents are to be found in junior classes. It tends to have the children from the poorer homes. The teachers themselves, none of whom comes from a pueblo joven, feel that they have in their school the dregs of society and some eloquently describe the problems encountered, and the inability of the children to learn. Such attitudes reinforce the fears of the parents; these are apparently justified by examples such as that of the child who was deemed by the Medalla Milagrosa school to have severe learning problems but who, on transfer to a private school, did extremely well.

The many children of Medalla Milagrosa who attend secondary school go outside the community, usually to one of the larger state schools in Magdalena del Mar. As we have seen, some of these have succeeded in reaching university, whilst others are preparing for the entrance examinations.

A small group of women in Medalla Milagrosa who have never received primary education – because they either grew up in a rural area poor in schooling, or were employed as domestic servants at an early age – attend a weekly literacy class in Medalla Milagrosa. They say that they want to learn so that they may be able to help their children with their lessons. Their own teacher is unqualified and thus his pupils cannot receive a certificate on completion of the course, a certificate which they could perhaps use in seeking employment.

Although Lima has so many agencies concerned with the development of the pueblos jóvenes, few of these seem to have any contact with Medalla Milagrosa, probably because of its small size. However, the nuns from the convent facing the settlement have taken a strong interest in the community. From an early period a few of them have been particularly involved in supplying food and clothing to the especially needy; this charitable work continues even now. But few of the pobladores are active church-goers, though all are nominally Catholic; nor do ceremonies of baptism or first communion play a large part in their lives. On the occasion of the annual patronal festival of the Virgin of the Medalla Milagrosa, several women spent a busy day decorating the image with flowers whilst a husband fixed the fairy lights; some youths carried the image to the church just over a kilometre away, for the evening service, but only a few children followed in the procession and hardly any pobladores attended the service. A few of the pobladores speak with approval of the efforts of the nuns; these tend to be the more affluent who have middle-class values or the very poor, the recipients of charity. The remainder view them with apathy or even with hostility.

With help from the Lions Club of Magdalena del Mar the building of the Club de Madres was started. A mothers' club is a typical feature of the pueblo joven, usually stimulated from outside and seen, by outsiders, as a forum for teaching the poor women the arts of household management, child-care and cooking. The club in Medalla Milagrosa was active for a short period, under the leadership of Señora Tuestas, an educated woman who works in the orphanage as a nurse. In 1975, it was defunct and critical comment was made by some concerning the disposal of its assets (some sewing-machines and cookers). When the nuns brought a team of adolescent girls from a middle-class Catholic youth club to clean up the club house, they were received with some polite apathy by the leaders of Medalla Milagrosa. During the period of our research a welfare agency organized a mid-afternoon series of lectures in the school, on children's problems; but only a small handful of women – not more than ten – attended. The Club de Madres had, in 1977, been resuscitated and was holding meetings on one afternoon each week. The total membership was said to exceed forty though only a quarter of this number were present at any one meeting; several nuns and lay helpers gave religious instruction and classes in domestic crafts.

Community activities such as fiestas organized by the pobladores themselves are much better supported. On one Sunday a *pachamanca* was held. This is a traditional sierra fiesta, though many in Medalla Milagrosa were witnessing it for the first time. Meat and vegetables, wrapped in leaves, are slowly cooked in an oven made by lining a pit with heated stones. In charge of preparing the food on this occasion was the community's wealthy trader; he had once worked in a restaurant and preserved an interest in cooking. Plates of the cooked food were sold for S/.100 a piece; drinks were available and the inevitable sapo tournament was held. The fiesta was organized by the governing committee in an effort to raise money for a fund from which would-be householders could borrow. As an event, providing entertainment, it was highly successful; but the money raised was small. The plates of food were too expensive for many pobladores: many a husband and wife shared a plate; the initial cost of the food was high, reducing the profit margin. It had been hoped that many outsiders would come, but little or no attempt at formal advertisement was made and the participants were, almost without exception, pobladores of Medalla Milagrosa. The fiesta, like so many church bazaars or village fêtes, was only a laborious way of taxing members of the community.

On another occasion, a fiesta was organized by the school's Parents' Committee to raise money for the electric lighting of the school. The kindergarten children, dressed in traditional costume, enacted plays about famous historical personages – Túpac Amaru and Batista – and performed indigenous dances. Plates of food – this time salads, at a cheaper price – and drink were available; and the four wards competed for the sapo cup. But again, few outsiders participated.

For the adolescents of Medalla Milagrosa there is no formal youth club. The boys and young men spend what free time they have playing football. Medalla Milagrosa has its own team, which recently came top of its league; and several youths play for the Lima team of their home village. The girls have no equivalent sport; in any case they tend to be much busier within the home. However, as was noted previously, at weekends a badminton net is erected at the entrance to the settlement and they and some of their male peers play together. Others sit idly on the wall, watching and chatting.

Such then is Medalla Milagrosa, the little pueblo joven in the cliffs. In the following chapters I take up two issues: the degree to which the settlement is a community, capable of collective action; and its relationship with the city, a relationship perhaps aptly described as one of 'marginality'.

5. Community

Medalla Milagrosa is not merely a locality, it is a community, in the everyday sense of that word. But the term community embraces a variety of traits; in what sense is Medalla Milagrosa a community? How far do its residents feel it to be one? To what extent are they willing and able to engage in communal activity? In a city where collective action is stressed one would expect a high level of activity in Medalla Milagrosa. But in recent years this has not been apparent; the people speak instead of a lack of will to work together, of weak leaders. Yet, when one considers such things as the house-building that is taking place, the success of the youths in reaching university and the frequent fiestas or street parties, one cannot attribute this lack of communal activity to apathy. In this chapter I shall explore the reasons for this recent lack of interest in Medalla Milagrosa and ask whether the factors which seem to be significant here are common in other pueblos jóvenes of similar size; for if they are, policies which aim to provide a social infrastructure – roads, electricity etc. – through collective action, or which aim to mobilize the population on the basis of small territorial units, must be seriously re-examined.

Medalla Milagrosa is a clearly defined territorial unit. Bounded by the sea and by high-class residential areas, it contrasts sharply to the surrounding areas. There is, in fact, no other near-by pueblo joven; Medalla Milagrosa is quite isolated. It is, however, officially recognized, and appears in maps and in statistics of Lima's pueblos jóvenes. It has, as we have seen, its own governing council of elected representatives whose task is to allocate land in the pueblo and regulate the building of houses, to collect charges for water and electricity and, in general, to promote the development of the community. For the residents the community council is one of their principal links with the national and municipal governments. Medalla Milagrosa has its own primary school and kindergarten, though many of its children attend school outside the pueblo; it has its own Club de Madres, its own football team. It is a moral community, in which the members express an obligation to maintain order. The governing council does not act formally as a judicial body; it works indirectly as a restraining force, and the presence of a policeman within Medalla Milagrosa is a rare occurrence.

The people of Medalla Milagrosa are very conscious of the hostility of the residents of the neighbouring estates, of the image of social disorganization, violence, crime and apathy, an image shared with the pobladores of other pueblos jóvenes. For two decades or more the residents of Medalla Milagrosa have successfully resisted attempts to evict and harrass them. In fact, they have won communal piped water, a domestic electricity supply and a rudimentary sewerage system. One might argue that these achievements should spur on the people of Medalla Milagrosa to even further activity to improve their community; though, equally, it might be felt that the effort and frustration experienced produces apathy.

As we already know the pobladores are linked by a network of kin relationships, and ties of godparenthood and marriage are subsequently created. These bonds are undoubtedly important in obviating feelings of isolation; those who might be scorned for their poverty or for their uncouth sierra habits find comfort in the fact that many of their neighbours behave as they do; they constitute a supportive reference group. Between close kin and neighbours there is clearly much practical help given in daily activities; but the dominant impression is of household independence. On one occasion when a child broke a leg and needed urgent hospital treatment, neighbours organized a collection to pay the hospital fees; but if a family is impoverished through unemployment, aid is given only in cases of extreme destitution. Friends and neighbours gossip at the water taps, but they spend little time entertaining each other within their homes.

Such leisure time as is available is spent within Medalla Milagrosa, but most often within the home itself. Many families now have a television set; this, it is alleged, has caused the marked decline in attendance at meetings of the governing council and of the general assembly of all the pobladores. The principal bar in Medalla Milagrosa is frequented less by residents than by downwardly mobile men from near-by residential areas.

Because so many of the people of Medalla Milagrosa work in the residential areas of the vicinity – as gardeners or domestics in the affluent homes, jobbing-builders or taxi-drivers, semi-skilled workers in the orphanage or mental hospital – they have a commitment to residence in Medalla Milagrosa; no other pueblo joven is so accessible; the alternative – renting rooms in a corralón – has already been rejected by them. Even those who work further afield have the advantage of a good bus service; they can reach the inner city more quickly than those living in Comas or Villa el Salvador. Some of the pobladores say that they would like to move away from Medalla Milagrosa giving as their reasons its squalor and the persistent gossip; others say that they prefer to live with their close kin or with people like themselves, and that the lower-class housing estate is cold and unfriendly. The people of Medalla Milagrosa certainly have a pride in their community. In a meeting with its university students I was asked at the outset how I saw the community – did I, they wondered, share the prevailing middle-class image? Yet when I answered that Medalla Milagrosa, in common with most pueblos jóvenes, was a community of hard-working, honest, law-abiding citizens, they protested that other settlements fully deserved the pejorative epithets customarily bestowed; Medalla Milagrosa, in contrast, was unusual in being so orderly and achievement-oriented. The loyalty of these youths seems significant because, on the verge of entering upon professional careers and thereby the middle classes, they could have so easily denigrated the slum into which, by chance, they had been born.

Medalla Milagrosa is a symbolic community; it provides emotional support for its members; it is a convenient and, by standards of other pueblos jóvenes, a fairly comfortable place in which to live. But it is not a community in an economic sense. Almost all men and women work outside the community; those who work at home, such as the tailor or the dressmaker, supply an external market. The little shops serve a local clientele almost exclusively, and their profits are thus derived from the community; yet most of the shopping is done outside, at suburban supermarkets or in the big street-market at Surquillo. Few people are active trade union members; most do not belong to a union nor to any organization of self-employed artisans or traders. Occupation does not, therefore, provide a basis for mobilization or collective action to any great extent.

The people of Medalla Milagrosa do not only have close kin living within the community, but they also have equally close relatives living elsewhere in Lima, especially in corralones or other pueblos jóvenes. Most commonly these are brothers and sisters, aunts, uncles and cousins, occasionally their own married children, but rarely their parents. Between such close kin, ties of affection and practical help remain very strong. We have noted earlier that many of the pobladores, though far from all, are members of a club pertaining to their place of birth. Such membership is most likely when the poblador comes from a small sierra village, from which the migrants have settled in relatively few localities in Lima and tend to enjoy a similar style of life, most being relatively poor and unskilled. Membership is less likely when the migrant comes from a provincial town, for the club will then be dominated by the local elite and he will feel excluded. There is no reason why a man should not participate both in his club and in communal activity in his pueblo joven; most of those who are active in Medalla Milagrosa are staunch members of their clubs too. Few of the pobladores in Medalla Milagrosa seem to be seriously contemplating a return to their natal home upon retirement; they are not investing their savings in a house at home instead of improving the one in Medalla Milagrosa. Yet, time is a scarce resource, and leadership within a club is incompatible with similar activity within the pueblo joven; money spent at a club fiesta, perhaps destined to furnish the village school, is not spent within Medalla Milagrosa for a like purpose.

Most descriptions of the shanty town stress the ethnic heterogeneity of the settlement; to the outside observer this is certainly their appearance. Yet in Lima the pueblo joven often contains groups of *paisanos* (compatriots); thus Medalla Milagrosa has a third of its families coming from Huancaray and in a bigger pueblo joven in Callao, Lobo (1977) found a large group originating from another Apurímac village – in this case living contiguously. Yet in Medalla Milagrosa, as in all probability in other pueblos jóvenes, most of the departments of Peru are represented. Such heterogeneity of origin is held to be a major deterrent to collective action; minor cultural differences, so obvious to the people themselves, contribute to social distancing and a lack of trust (cf. Roberts 1973). Yet one would expect that two decades of co-residence would break down such barriers even though continued allegiance to the home area, through the club, maintains this ethnic segregation.

In Medalla Milagrosa there are few families of criollo origin; yet the stereotypes of criollo and sierra behaviour are widely accepted. The sierra family works very hard, lives poorly and invests in education; the criollo family lives more for the present, spends more on house furnishing. Abuse of the poor (from all sectors) within Medalla Milagrosa is frequently in ethnic terms: 'they have the dirty habits of the sierra Indian'. Some informants suggested that a more marked division existed between those who came from backward villages, such as Huancaray, and those who had grown up in urban areas, whether in the sierra or on the coast. This may well parallel a division between the upwardly mobile – those from poor villages who now enjoy better housing, piped water and electricity – and the downwardly mobile – those from urban homes but now resident in a marginal settlement. Such social and cultural divisions do not equate well with physical distinctions; most people from the sierra villages of the mancha india do have a markedly Indian appearance, but those who are white in complexion come from a wide range of origins. (Such has been the racial mixing in Peru through the centuries that children in a middle-class mestizo family often vary quite strikingly in colour and appearance.)

In everyday activities none of these distinctions seems pronounced. The elder son of a criollo family has recently married a young sierra woman. A negro resident is comparatively active in communal affairs. In a meeting of the Club de Madres, the members, though all of sierra origin, ranged from quite white to Indian in appearance; the former were more active in talking to the nuns (all white, some of recent Spanish origin) but the latter only participated fully when the members began to discuss their recent fiesta among themselves. Apart from organizing the Christmas festival of *Los Negritos*, the Huancaray families did not seem to operate as a block, though we searched hard for such a division. Nor did there appear to be other permanent structural divisions, such as factions grouped around rival leaders. The most significant division was that imposed by SINAMOS in the creation of four local wards, representatives from which make up the governing council; the effect of this will be discussed below. This territorial grouping of the pobladores bears not the slightest relationship to any ethnic or social divisions.

The most marked distinction in Medalla Milagrosa lies between its richer and its poorer families, and it is here that heterogeneity in the population is significant, as the later sections of this chapter will illustrate.

Finally, in posing the question 'how far is Medalla Milagrosa a community?', we have focused attention on activity at one level – that of the territorial locality; perhaps higher or lower units are more significant. Thus, in her study of a small shanty town in the heart of Mexico City, Lomnitz (1977) shows that the residents belong to a number of small networks of kin and neighbours and that these networks are highly significant in their daily behaviour; in contrast the community as a whole does not act collectively; it has no governing council or activities such as have been described for Medalla Milagrosa. Kin groupings are undoubtedly strong within Medalla Milagrosa, but it does exist as a community. But, there is no larger unit – a grouping of pueblos jóvenes, for instance – to which the pobladores of Medalla Milagrosa owe any allegiance.

Community needs and action

Medalla Milagrosa seems deserving of the designation 'community'. Were its people to come from a much more restricted area, to engage in similar economic activities, to be less differentiated in wealth and concomitant life-styles, it would be a more pronounced community. Yet it is unlikely that any of the small pueblos jóvenes in Lima has these characteristics; nor are the larger ones likely to display them. So, if Medalla Milagrosa is unable to generate collective activity, it seems unlikely that other similar settlements will be able to do so. Many of the perceived needs of the people, it is true, are seen as capable of individual solution: the building of one's house, finding a better job, educating one's children. Yet communal needs are continually being stressed; the pobladores want legal title to their property, houses and land; they would like water piped into their homes (thus enabling them to have a better sewerage system); they ask for the tarring of the central road and the provision of street-lighting; they would like to beautify the entrance of the pueblo with grass verges and flowering trees and to develop little plazas at the junction of the road and the upper passage, and halfway down the road, around the shrine. To the outside observer none of these needs seems to pose insuperable problems, and his immediate reponse would be that, with collective effort, the people could achieve their goals; if they cannot achieve them, it is evidence of their apathy or ineptitude.

These attitudes are reinforced when the dominant policies and ideologies of the state favour development through collective action, when self-help programmes are fostered by the government, lauded in the press and believed by the mass of the poor to be the means by which they can attain higher standards of living. The people of Medalla Milagrosa ascribe their lack of the services cited above, not to a failure of the Peruvian government to provide them, but to their own inability to act collectively.

The voluntary agencies which have been so active in the barriadas of Lima have sought variously to provide basic services so as to ameliorate the conditions of poverty, to instil into the migrant poor the dominant middle-class values in the society, to educate an apathetic mass to appreciate that it can (to a greater extent than apparently realized) control its own destiny. The efforts of those agencies have been vigorously opposed by radical politicians and intellectuals, but primarily in terms of the goals sought; for they too would wish to see the poor mobilized, though in what they conceive to be their own interests rather than those of the dominant classes. The self-help programmes of these agencies tend to be directed towards limited short-term goals: that is, to secure the provision of a single service. State schemes tend to involve long-term goals of improvement; here it is becoming increasingly accepted that popular participation is the key factor in the success of the projects; the state cannot expect to impose its plans, however praiseworthy, upon a populace unable or unwilling to appreciate the benefits conferred.

These current perspectives in development are reflected in the objectives of SINAMOS. Through this vast state apparatus, the demands of the poor for urban services and the ability of the state to provide them, given its other policies and commitments, have been mediated. The state lacks the ability to meet all the demands made, but its resources are supplemented by the voluntary labour of the recipients, who are, in effect, taxing themselves heavily to provide the service. Through these collective efforts the poor are encouraged to feel that they are in control of their lives and living conditions; just as in the industrial community, the social property enterprise or the co-operative, they would appear to control the organization in which they are employed. Such efforts at social mobilization have, however, their inherent dangers; development may become too fast, chaotic and unplanned; the masses, revelling in the attention paid to them, begin to make demands beyond the limits which the government is prepared to accede. SINAMOS was thus an agent of control, restricting the development of the pueblos jóvenes to an acceptable speed and direction, and curbing the militancy of the popular leaders. It thus recruited to its ranks both the radical idealists, who saw an opportunity for useful service to the poor, and the more authoritarian bureaucrat. In its early years when it was attempting to stimulate activity in the pueblos jóvenes, and when the government had considerable funds to allocate to infrastructural projects, SINAMOS had a progressive image. Latterly the element of control has predominated, with the agency seen in many settlements as a force impeding desired development, and in extremes, its agents viewed as police spies tracking down any signs of militancy and disaffection.

Yet, even in the more favourable climate of the early 1970s, the people of Medalla Milagrosa collectively achieved little. But what did their statements, that they were unco-operative or that their leaders were ineffective, really mean? Were they merely statements of fact or did they mask their own reluctance to act? As already indicated, apathy seems to be no answer – for the efforts at house-building and in education and the organization of fiestas seem to indicate a lively and active population.

The situation described in Medalla Milagrosa is far from unique; in fact much of the literature on the squatter settlements not only of Lima but also of other South American cities notes that communal activity decreases with the age of the community; none suggests a contrary trend. As Dietz (1977a) argues for Lima, one cannot attribute this to the personality of the residents of the older pueblo joven for the same people have successively lived in a corralón (with no communal activity at all), invaded land, organized their settlement and now live in a well-established community. It has been suggested that as a settlement ages so the demands of the people become those to be met by individual rather than collective action; yet very few settlements have so little to be achieved by collective action that their activity should fall to such a minimal level.

Medalla Milagrosa, nearly 20 years old, still has its list of pressing needs. The later demands, it is suggested, may be more complex, more difficult to achieve than earlier ones; but there is little evidence that this is so. It is probable that in its earlier years a settlement receives more attention from outside bodies and that its activity reflects this external input; Medalla Milagrosa was able to make political capital from its subjection to the effects of the stone-crushing machine, and some of its services seem to have been provided as a consolation for the suffering caused. Again, in the early years, the threat of eviction is greater, and people will mobilize more readily in the face of such a threat; the initial provision of services is seen as a symbol of legitimacy. None of these arguments, however, seems to be entirely convincing.

In most of the discussion of communal activity it is implied that there exists in a community a general propensity to act collectively, this being adduced either by measurement of the level of activity or by the expression of attitudes. Firstly, the nature of a particular given task – the resources needed to accomplish it – is rarely considered, with the result that two communities may be compared in the performance of very different tasks. Secondly, the community is presented as homogeneous; the range of divergent interests – and the degree to which these are promoted by any specific development – are not discussed. Most discussions of the effect of the 'Green Revolution' – the introduction of new high-yield crop varieties – now admit that it favours the rich farmers at the expense of the poor; that the former, for instance, are active in promoting co-operatives which grant them credit. Such differential benefits are yet to be as widely discussed in the context of urban development. In assessing the level of collective activity one must ask what it is that the community is trying to do.

As the community ages, the range of 'apparent' socio-economic variation widens: 'apparent' because at the birth of the settlement some will have more savings than others, some will be in better-paid and more stable jobs; yet all live in small estera huts. With time, some families build imposing houses, some get their children into university. This differentiation, for the reasons I shall develop at the end of this chapter, leads to an increasing individualism. Thus, it is not that the most felt needs become more individual than collective, but that the attitudes taken towards all needs become infused with an individualism which inhibits collective activity.

In this chapter I look specifically at Medalla Milagrosa. Many of the factors which seem to inhibit or promote collective activity will be unique to this settlement; others, however, will be of general application. I believe also that one cannot explain activity, or its absence, in terms of one or two factors; the process is a highly complex one. It is difficult enough to list the operative factors, but it is harder to assess the degree to which a weakness in one factor may be compensated for by strength elsewhere; thus good leadership may be desirable – but how far can poor leadership be offset by ethnic homogeneity, for example? Again, collective activity towards given goals is a synchronic process; just as one must get the numbers in the right order to open a safe, so too must the various inputs into a development project be provided in the correct sequence. Long-term projects, for instance, are apt to flounder when the achievement of the ultimate goal remains problematic and no immediate rewards are granted in compensation.

Let us look, therefore, at some of the associations and services that the people of Medalla Milagrosa seek to develop, asking, in turn, what benefits they are likely to bring, who will benefit, what costs are incurred, what resources needed. Medalla Milagrosa seems in this respect a typical pueblo joven. In a survey of needs expressed in 1967 by barriada residents throughout Lima, Andrews and Phillips (1970) found that the demand for property titles and near-by medical services was most intense, though not exceptionally widespread, for many of those questioned already had titles. Street-paving was desired by almost all, though not so urgently. Water, street-lighting, sewerage, a post office, a police post were all sought both intensively and by a majority of pobladores. Low in demand were schools, and credit for housing; the need for schools was not so pressing because so many children attended institutions in the adjacent suburbs, credit because most people preferred to use their own savings as and when available. Intermediate needs were local associations, parks and recreation areas, churches and public transportation. At present some of these items are not actively sought by the people of Medalla Milagrosa because they already have access to them; for instance, a good bus service, near-by secondary schools, a church. The things which they do seek rank high, however, in the list presented by Andrews and Phillips.

Apart from its governing committees, the Club de Madres is the premier association of Medalla Milagrosa; yet it was inactive for several years in the early 1970s and no progress was made in completing its building. The purpose of the club, as seen both by its leading members and by the nuns who actively assist in running it, is to give the women an opportunity to get together to discuss common problems and to 'improve' themselves. At the weekly afternoon meetings the nuns give religious instruction while their lay helpers instruct in cookery and needlework. With the reopening of the Club in late 1976, nearly forty women registered, though the average attendance at a meeting is about ten. The president is Señora Tuestas, wife of the leader of Medalla Milagrosa in the late 1960s, and herself a comparatively well-educated woman, with a stable and responsible job in the near-by orphanage. At times in the meetings she refers to the other women as my 'comadres'; several are related to her in this way and represent to some extent a personal following. It seems that the problems of Medalla Milagrosa – its property titles, its sewerage – are not widely discussed in the meetings; in any case there would seem to be no channels through which demands could be articulated by the club. A few women are members of the governing committees and many attend general assemblies or lobbying visits to government offices, especially when these take place during the day, and they represent their husbands who cannot leave their work. Our interviews disclosed that women were, in most cases, well able to discuss the pueblo's problems. The main function of the Club de Madres seems, therefore, to be an avenue for a few women to display their higher social status in the community.

The tarring of the road is sought mainly by those with well-furnished houses and who are most disturbed by the dust thrown up by the occasional passing vehicle; for the only motor traffic on the road are the lorries delivering soft drinks to the little canteens, the taxi and truck owned by individual pobladores, and the occasional taxi or private car bringing visitors. Those with good houses often throw their waste soapy water onto the road to settle the dust, and very occasionally collect water from the stand-pipe specifically for this purpose. Most people, however, close their windows and tolerate the dust, often not noticing it in the general unitidiness of the home. To tar the road would be quite a major operation. The road needs to be levelled, but this could be achieved by communal labour; the tarmac surfacing would have to be provided by an outside contractor; for the building of pavements each householder would need to work extensively on the frontage of his home to align it with the new level. In all, tarring the road would demand much labour and financial expenditure.

One reason for demanding street-lights is that thieves who rob houses in the adjacent residential areas would be deterred from entering Medalla Milagrosa to evade capture or recognition. For the residents, street-lighting is a relative luxury, for no one fears to walk in the street at night; however, it is a symbol of the pueblo's development. Beyond digging holes for the standards there is little that the people can do themselves; the new service must be obtained through the electricity company and paid for; this would probably involve a down payment of a substantial proportion of the cost, with the remainder repaid, with interest, in instalments collected with the other local rates.

Most people would clearly prefer to have water piped into their homes; but few could bear the costs involved. Though the water would presumably be drawn from the main supply running along Avenida del Ejército at the entrance to the pueblo, the existing pipes through the settlement are too small to cope with the greater demand. Again, much of the work would have to be carried out by the water company.

Spurred on by the sight of municipal labourers planting and frequently watering the verges in the adjacent residential areas, the pobladores have renewed their efforts to beautify the entrance to the settlement. Here the technical problems seem slight and no outside help is needed; the gardeners can get grass and cuttings for planting. But the nearest stand-pipe is many yards away at a much lower level; even if a hose were available the water pressure would be insufficient, and so the plants must be watered by bucket. Recently a short hose has been donated and the water tapped near the entrance. One youth started working regularly on the verges but stopped when others did not co-operate. Meanwhile the new shrubs struggle to survive.

Property titles

The main issue, which has been dominating discussion in the governing council during the past two years, has been the acquisition of property titles. The people of Medalla Milagrosa compare themselves and their leaders unfavourably with those of other, often much newer, pueblos jóvenes which have gained legal title. To a great extent the demand is stimulated by the government itself; in granting titles it further legalizes the existence of the pueblos jóvenes and so engenders popularity. The grant of title and administrative procedure is relatively cheap, involving none of the technical problems raised in supplying water, electricity or sewerage; furthermore, it provides additional employment for middle-class bureaucrats. For the people of Medalla Milagrosa, the grant of a title is the ultimate safeguard against eviction.

In much of the literature on shanty towns it is argued that lack of title impedes investment in housing. In Medalla Milagrosa very few people say that they have not built a better house because they feel insecure; there is no obvious spending elsewhere, so one concludes that this statement is only a cover for their poverty. Certainly others have been building in the belief that as the quality of housing improves, so is the likelihood reduced that bulldozers will be sent to eradicate the settlement. Legal title will, of course, make the transfer of property easier (the buying and selling of houses in pueblos jóvenes has existed without title being granted; but with the greater surveillance by SINAMOS to prevent multiple owner-ship and speculation it became more difficult to do so). But few wish to sell their property; it will be inherited by their children who, hopefully, will not fight each other in the courts for a larger share. Title is also necessary to get credit, but as we have seen, few men seek this. In addition, title could be a prerequisite for the installation of costly services, as the public service corporations need to know exactly who is liable to repay the debts incurred.

The granting of title involves the whole community, not simply those who feel in greatest need of the legal documents. Necessary preliminaries in Medalla Milagrosa were the preparation of two plans by a qualified surveyor, one being a contoured plan of the area, and the other showing the boundaries of each property. The cost of these falls entirely on the community. (It had been suggested that university students of engineer-ing might prepare the plans as a class project, but nothing came of this.) A further prerequisite is the remodelling of the settlement, for title will not be granted for properties which are sited in an irregular manner. In some pueblos jóvenes, remodelling involves the complete clearance of the area with some of the population resettled on the newly laid out plots, the remainder moved elsewhere. In Medalla Milagrosa the houses face the street in an even fashion; the frontages are approximately equal; but, due to the nature of the gully, some have been extended much further in depth; these houses in consequence are larger. In contrast the houses and plots above the upper passage are small. In replanned settlements the maximum size of plot has been reduced from 120 square metres to 90 square metres, an area much smaller than the large Medalla Milagrosa plots. Those in the community with the larger plots fear that some of their land might be taken from them, though they anticipate that a well-constructed house will be left untouched, whatever its size. However, they are opposed in the community by a vocal minority protesting that some owners with small plots cannot build houses large enough to accommodate a growing family, that tenants of long standing are unable to acquire their own plots, all because some greedy owners of large plots will not release land. (It is difficult to see how they might release land, for there is no vacant land fronting the street; any unused land lies at the back of the house and would be unsuitable for an independent dwelling.)

A further problem lies in the sewerage of Medalla Milagrosa which is at present washed by waste-water to an effluence in the cliffs. The municipality of Magdalena del Mar is becoming increasingly interested in extending the *costa verde* – the promenade and its attendant beach attractions – through its own territory. In this situation the sewerage outfall is clearly too obnoxious to be tolerated. Yet it seems to be accepted that the rectification of the problem lies with Medalla Milagrosa and not with the municipality; and that while the settlement continues to cause a public nuisance in this way, its tolerated acceptance in its present site will remain in doubt. (A further threat to the settlement lies in the recent – August 1977 – announcement that the orphanage and mental hospital are to be moved to new buildings on the edge of the city and that on the land so vacated a residential complex of 4,000 flats, shops etc. will be constructed. The people of Medalla Milagrosa profess not to be unduly worried by this.)

The preparation of the existing plans has already necessitated the collection of more than S/.1,000 from each household; some leaders estimate that the total costs of the operation will exceed S/.15,000, or almost three months' pay at a minimum wage.

Causes of failure

From this survey it would seem that the services demanded are either luxuries of benefit to only a few, or amenities necessary to all, which would be excessively costly; yet the demands are made and the people make at least some effort to achieve their stated goals. We must therefore pursue our enquiry into their apparent failure. Do they, one asks, make the correct moves, only to be faced with an inefficient or intransigent bureaucracy upon which the blame should rightly lie? Or can the failures be attributed to the quality of leadership in Medalla Milagrosa, the nature of the demands made of individual house-holders, or their growing individualism?

Outside agencies

As we have said, there is a great deal that the people of Medalla Milagrosa could do for themselves: they could run the Club de Madres; they could plant shrubs at the entrance of the settlement; but all their major needs – title, water, electricity, sewerage – demand the extensive co-operation of government agencies with respect to financing, technical assistance and the ultimate supply of the service. How does each party view the other? What are their respective expectations and demands?

For the people of Medalla Milagrosa, the issues of title and remodelling are not new and they approach the current situation with some disillusion. In the early 1960s an engineer promised to help them with a redevelopment scheme but this, so the people believe, was quashed by the wealthy landowners who did not wish to see the settlement become increasingly stable. Throughout the decade, Medalla Milagrosa, for good technical reasons, was decreed 'eradicable'; in an earthquake there would be considerable danger to property and life from land-falls. Plans were submitted at the end of the 1960s but to no effect.

In November 1975 a meeting was held in the SINAMOS office when officials explained to a large number of pobladores the nature of the process involved and the plans that were needed. The ball was placed definitely in the Medalla Milagrosa court. The response of the pobladores developed into an attack on the community leaders by a small minority who sought larger plots or who were trying to establish a right to land seized against the consent of the governing council; the officials recommended that the pobladores go home and set their house in order.

Medalla Milagrosa leaders report that individual officials whom they meet are courteous and helpful; this is an image which SINAMOS had tried to convey. But the officials, whose resources are limited, are faced with requests from many settlements. They tend to favour communities such as Villa el Salvador where their development projects take the form of a vast public relations exercise. Small communities such as Medalla Milagrosa get left behind, for projects here bring little prestige either to the organization or to individual officials. SINAMOS was, furthermore, expected by the government to ensure an orderly development of services; technical standards must be maintained: the installation of water pipes, for example, must not outrun the available supply. Many of the officials in government departments and agencies are young and inexperienced and tend to follow bureaucratic procedures literally. The effect of this situation is that officials will act only when the applicants have gone through all the expected motions. They do not visit the community to help the pobladores with these; and least of all do they recommend to them methods of evading, bypassing or cutting corners. Instead they expect the applicants to lobby them in their offices, thus accepting the finding of so many social scientists that the only way for the poor to succeed is by making a nuisance of themselves, and action is easier than stalling. One SINAMOS official said that the people of Medalla Milagrosa – with one exception – lobbied him much less than those of other pueblos jóvenes, and as a result got less attention.

But the people of Medalla Milagrosa, whilst recognizing this principle, are neither unemployed nor in such secure employment that they can take time off for such lobbying. They see only the complexity of the process (difficult even for the educated to comprehend) and vainly try one official after another in an attempt to find a way through the maze. They feel, with probable justification, that the government departments are inefficient; leaders of Medalla Milagrosa suspect that a ministry had mislaid their papers; the experiences of other settlements are common knowledge (in the remodelled settlement in Callao studied by Lobo (1976), water, electricity and titles were still awaited three years after the site had been bulldozed and settlers allocated their new plots). In recent years the image of SINAMOS deteriorated. It was associated with forced eviction of settlers in certain pueblos jóvenes (in one case in 1977 those evicted occupied a city church in protest); with the growing militancy among the poor in the economic recession of the mid-1970s, SINAMOS agents were seen as police spies; stories circulated about assaults against officials which resulted in the widespread arrest of community leaders. The governing councils recognized by SINAMOS were matched in some pueblos jóvenes by alternative councils apparently representing more popular views.

In this atmosphere of increasing repression and fear, it is understandable that the pobladores mute their protests and behave with the utmost correctness. In their more pessimistic moments the leaders of Medalla Milagrosa say that they are afraid of being deceived by the government agencies; that the hope of gaining title is only a ploy to keep them happy; that once again nothing will happen as the application for title will fail on some legal technicality; that Medalla Milagrosa will be eradicated one day. Yet they do not give up the struggle but, according to their ability, continue to press their claims. On the other hand the young woman from Medalla Milagrosa responsible for the actual negotiations with SINAMOS reported that its officials have been correct and helpful and that the next move is for the community to make: that is, they must engage professionals to prepare the remodelling plans.

To an outside observer, hopefully impartial, it would appear that although the government and its agencies impose difficult tasks on the pobladores of Medalla Milagrosa and similar pueblos jóvenes in their attempts to achieve their goals, failure lies in the inability of the community to mobilize to a sufficient degree. Since the leaders of the community are responsible for the attainment of these goals, the failure is theirs. Yet we must distinguish between their personal weaknesses and the intractable problems set for them in maintaining the support of their electorate.

Leadership

The leader of the pueblo joven requires two types of resource: he must have the respect of the people so that they obey his call to pay contributions, to provide communal labour and to accept his decisions about land allocation; and he must be effective in dealing with the bureaucracy so that his community gets the services it needs. From the literature of squatter settlements two ideal types of leader emerge. One is the wealthy man, probably an entrepreneur and probably relatively well educated. His success is widely admired; he is a role model for others in his community. He serves his community largely for altruistic motives; he belongs to many associations, and these, as well as his office as leader, contribute to his continuing success. He has many contacts outside the settlement and these he exploits for the benefit of his people. When he is accused of using his position for self-aggrandizement he retires from the political arena, but continues to be successful and influential.

The other type of leader is the 'ward boss'. He is a demagogue, possibly poorly educated and in unstable employment. He wins the recognition of officials because he can ensure the support required; he retains his following because he can intercede with officials and attain the required favours; his brokerage role demands that his following is prevented from directly contacting the officials, and it is from this role that he may well derive his main income. Kiboro, in Ross' (1973) account of the Mathare Valley settlement in Nairobi, and the *caciques* of Mexico City described by Cornelius (1975), are good examples of this type of leader. Such a leader has never emerged in Medalla Milagrosa probably because it is too small to maintain this type of person, although Señor Tuestas, leader of Medalla Milagrosa from 1967 to 1971, had many of the qualities of the respected worthy citizen.

In a survey of leadership in barriadas in Lima, Paredes (1973) has suggested a progression through three types of leader: there is the charismatic figure who organizes the invasion; he is followed by an able man more concerned with the developmental goals of the community; then once these are attained, the leaders are men of limited skills who are required merely to supervise the routine daily administration of the community. It is tempting to see this progression in Medalla Milagrosa, though here it has perhaps been produced as an effect of the SINAMOS pattern of government rather than as a natural development.

The constitution of the 'Asociación de Pobladores' was altered as SINAMOS imposed its own pattern on all the pueblos jóvenes. First, politically active persons were debarred from office; this did not affect anyone in Medalla Milagrosa (and in any case membership of political parties was at a very low ebb in the early and mid-1970s); the intention of SINAMOS was to make the community councils representative of the mass of the people and to inhibit the development of militancy. Secondly, offices were to be held for two years only, an office-holder being ineligible for re-election (though he could hold another office). This seems to be an attempt to spread the tasks of leadership as widely as possible, to involve a large number in the government of their community; but it, too, detracts from the development of skilled and powerful leadership. The SINAMOS hierarchy extended from its central office, through its branches, down to the individual blocks in the squatter settlement. We know that Medalla Milagrosa was divided into four committees, in each of which the office-holders elected the central committee. Here again SINAMOS gave as its justification the political involvement of the greater number, and the benefits of inter-committee competition.

In practice, the pobladores saw the system as a disaster. Decision making became protracted as everything had to be discussed by the four committees and the central committee, and perhaps by a general meeting of the people. It was not clear whether initiatives should come from the top or the bottom; SINAMOS officials said from the top, but the central committee members were then accused of being autocratic. The secretary general of the central committee found it difficult to keep in touch with the four committees. Rivalry among the four committees fostered independence; ill-feeling was created when the four committees were expected to contribute equally, yet some had fewer households than others. Suspicions and accusations about misuse of funds led the committees to establish their own bank accounts. One ward had more of the active pobladores than others (and this, incidentally embraced the upper passage with its poorer houses); the other committees resented its initiative. SINAMOS officials recognized the problems which their structure had caused, but waited for a move by Medalla Milagrosa. This was not forthcoming because the remission of committee independence could not be unanimously agreed.

The first leader in Medalla Milagrosa was Señor Laura, the longest-established resident after the departure of Señor Flores. He is now an elderly man in his final years of employment as a labourer in the Magdalena del Mar municipality. He is of sierra Indian origin and has little education. He is, however, admired not only for the power which he wielded in the initial allocation of plots but also for his tenacity in resisting the eradication of the settlement. He is a stolid, hard-working man, a typical serrano, who has set high standards for his children with considerable success. He is said to have many contacts outside Medalla Milagrosa, but the more influential ones probably derive from his leadership position; others are the consequence of long residence and the clientele of his bar.

Señor Tuestas was leader for the four years during which period Medalla Milagrosa gained many of its services. One cannot tell how far these were the consequence of external intervention or of the part played by Tuestas; he was certainly a very active worker and his efforts are recorded in the testimonials which decorate the walls of his living room, and the title 'Alcalde' with which the pobladores greet him. He comes from a relatively prosperous and religious peasant family in the northern sierra department of Amazonas. He is better educated than most of his age group and has a stable and well-paid white-collar job in a university library. He is, therefore, more adroit than others in Medalla Milagrosa in negotiating with officials and benefactors, and in finding his way through bureaucratic corridors. As we already know, his wife, also well educated, is president of the Club de Madres; together they constitute a strong team. In recent years he has worked on late afternoon–evening shift and so has had mornings free for public activities. Time, and the financial resources to pay many expenses out of his own pocket, are invaluable assets to a leader. At the end of the 1960s, with the campaign against the stone-crushing machine at its height, and with the pobladores developing their settlement through communal labour, Medalla Milagrosa was continually in the news, especially in the more ephemeral papers dealing with barriada affairs; in most of the reports Tuestas' name was juxtaposed with those of dignitaries and benefactors. The position of Señor and Señora Tuestas in Medalla Milagrosa was reinforced by the ties of godparenthood established with many families. Accusations were nevertheless levelled against the Tuestas' that they were using their positions for personal benefit. Clearly their careers were not advanced; they hold the same posts now as before 1967; the claims made seem rather trivial: that in the remodelling plans of the late 1960s, a street-light was to be outside their house; that the open space in front of their house, long in existence, was to be made into a little plaza; and that sewing-machines donated for the community were kept in the Tuestas' house (in the absence of a club house) and used only by Señora Tuestas and her friends.

However, most people still speak well of Señor Tuestas; but in a manner typical of ex-leaders he seems to have opted out of the day-to-day government of the community, though with Señor Laura, he was a prominent speaker at the SINAMOS meeting of November 1975.

The next three leaders have each held office for the statutory two years: Señor Inga, a retired policeman; Señor Porras, a driver in a construction company; and Señor Huamalie then the owner of Medalla Milagrosa's most prosperous provisions shop. All put a very great effort into their task though their capacities differed widely. Inga identified more closely with the wealthier and more educated pobladores; he was meticulous in his care of finances and decried the allegedly atrocious book-keeping which he inherited. He was apt to be officious in his dealings with others; he tells how, in fulfilling a directive from the Ministry of Education to provide the numbers of Medalla Milagrosa children at school inside and outside the settlement, he got into trouble with the pobladores who argued that this should have been publicly discussed. Porras and Huamalie are typical sierra Indians from poor remote villages. Porras is from Huancaray and is at the forefront in all communal activities, encouraging others by his own efforts. Huamalie is a more extrovert and gregarious individual whose term of office was marred by the sickness of his wife, the consequent collapse of his business, and his failing eyesight. These tragedies prevented him from giving as much attention as he might to his office. Each of these three men, though able to maintain a following among the people, was incapable of fulfilling the broker's role: they had little education, few influential contacts and very little time and financial resources to devote to their tasks. Their short time in office inhibited the development of their leadership roles.

The book-keeping procedures of these leaders, and of other committee members, are most rudimentary and it is perhaps not surprising that there are continual allegations of peculation, although clearly no one is making any substantial gains. However, in a small community, such gossip can be far more damaging: one household head now works far from Lima because he was accused of misappropriating community funds. (Beliefs of corruption are not entirely without foundation; Lobo (1976) reports that in her Callao community the organizers of a building fund, absconded with the money.)

The position of the leaders in recent years has been weakened by their inability to get committee members to attend meetings; they plead pressures of work. Disillusionment with the leadership further inhibits co-operation. Many of the more prosperous men say rather piously that they feel that the leadership demands considerable time and effort if it is to be successful, and they are not prepared to deprive their work or their families in this way; yet those who do assume office have even less ability to give time and resources to it. The various tasks assumed by office-holders – planning community development and the routine collection of fees – could well constitute a full-time job for one or two people; yet the ethos of community development in general, and of SINAMOS in particular, is that these tasks should be performed voluntarily and widely distributed.

Furthermore, the leaders and their committees have no sanctions with which to coerce people. When the pobladores failed to attend a general assembly to discuss electricity payments, it was suggested, but more in jest, that the current be switched off at the entrance to the pueblo so that they might be driven from their television sets. Some householders refuse to pay their electricity bills; the rates charged are artificially raised to cover such default, much to the chagrin of the honest; yet nobody is ever disconnected for this would cause too much ill-feeling between kin and neighbours, and damage existing relationships. The water supply of Medalla Milagrosa is metered; but there seems to be little that leaders can do to prevent costly wastage by those who leave the taps open, or to make those who run a hose from the tap to their own storage tanks pay an increased fee.

The leaders have even lost control over building within the pueblo. The area at the junction of the upper passage and the street has always been intended as a little plaza although no development has taken place. A woman, given a licence to erect a temporary house on this site, built instead a brick house; even more flagrantly, her sister rebuilt the adjacent squalid hut of her father in spite of vocal protests; her stepfather, a prominent committee member and a mason, helped in erecting the rein-forced concrete pillars, demonstrating the predominance of kin ties over those of community. These sisters claimed that their building was permitted by SINAMOS, thus overriding the community ruling.

With the formal leadership so weak one looks for alternative foci of influence and power. Medalla Milagrosa has no poblador of outstanding wealth or success; there are several who, by local standards, are moderately well off, but though they are respected and have some influence, they work hard and are too preoccupied with their jobs and their families to play a very effective role. One young woman, however, has played an extremely active role in the land title issue.

Yolanda Félix is the daughter of Medalla Milagrosa's poorest inhabitant who now collects empty cement bags and similar rubbish for recycling; her mother owns a small shop in Medalla Milagrosa; her parents are now separated, but both continue to live in the community with their new spouses. Señorita Félix, as she was known, attended a teacher-training college and was a student activist; as a result of student protests she (in common with others) failed to be awarded a certificate. Briefly she attended university. She became a committee member and was severely critical of the other leaders. She then went to Guatemala and established a reputation as a singer on television. She returned to Medalla Milagrosa in late 1975 and for the next two years devoted herself to its affairs, having no other local job. Her first move was to rebuild her father's house, defying the community prohibition described above; her position was further weakened inasmuch as she claimed that the house was to be in her own name, yet only household heads can hold land and she was an unmarried daughter. Furthermore, she drove out the wife of her father, obliging her to seek refuge in Villa el Salvador. All this provoked much hostility in Medalla Milagrosa and predicated Señorita Félix's outburst at the SINAMOS meeting, when she accused the leaders of denying land to the needy, while they had substantial houses.

Nevertheless, Señorita Félix was given, by the central committee, a co-optive office and charged with organizing the application for title to land; and it is she who had most of the dealings with SINAMOS and other officials, and who was recognized by them as the spokesman for Medalla Milagrosa. She seems to have established a good rapport with them. But to an equal degree she antagonized the people of Medalla Milagrosa. Not only did her highhanded building efforts rankle, but her continuing abuse of the leaders for their stupidity and laziness won no friends. At committee meetings she dominated the proceedings whilst the men, tired from a hard day's work, fell asleep or drifted home. Many women still refer to her using the rather derogatory nickname which she had as a small child.

The university students in Medalla Milagrosa play a relatively passive role. They are able youths and their sophistication contrasts markedly with the dour simplicity of their parents. Their loyalty to the community is impressive. Technically they are not allowed to hold office, this being reserved for household heads; but that alone seems insufficient to account for their inactivity. They do say that they feel seriously constrained when speaking in public in the presence of their parents; they see their own educational success as a means whereby they can lift their entire families out of poverty and they do not wish to alienate their elders in any way. Furthermore, they have little time: they work throughout the day to support themselves and pay their fees, and they attend classes and lectures in the evening. Even so, one such student has held office in his district club, saying that he felt that he could contribute and achieve more there than was possible in Medalla Milagrosa. These students are fully cognizant of all the radical rhetoric current in student circles, and some of them accept its tenets; yet none is politically active; in fact, they seem to avoid involvement in order that their studies and future careers should not be jeopardized. Thus, whilst some can analyse the situation of Medalla Milagrosa in radical terms, they do not translate their beliefs into action. Nor, in particular, did they give even overt support to Señorita Félix.

Equality of benefit

One explanation for the failure of the leaders of Medalla Milagrosa and for those of other pueblos jóvenes is that, in insisting upon a principle of equality of contribution in a community so clearly differentiated in wealth, they are set an almost impossible task.

It still seems a cardinal tenet in so much community development literature that development usually benefits all people, if not exactly equally, at least to a considerable degree. Until this decade it was similarly assumed that national economic development was advantageous to all; now it is accepted that growth usually leads to greater social inequalities. But services do appear to benefit rich and poor alike. All share in drinking water from a tap rather than from that brought in a tanker and stored in an open drum. The corollary of this view is that all should contribute equally; each household or each adult should perform the same amount of communal labour; each household should make an equal contribution towards the rates levied.

This concept of equality is held by the leaders and people of Medalla Milagrosa. It is as if the marked differences in wealth are seen as so threatening to community solidarity that measures are taken to reinforce the ideal of equality. The governing councils, the fiestas – and equality of contribution – are all seen as strengthening cohesion within Medalla Milagrosa. The committees did in fact debate a suggestion that the costs of preparing the plans in the application for property titles should be collected according to a graduated scale, but decided in principle against this. So whilst each household is metered for electricity and so pays only for what it consumes (technically a simple procedure), a uniform levy is made for water, and the periodic collections of S/.1,000 or S/.2,000 (5½–11 days' minimum wage) fall equally on each household.

Such large sums are clearly beyond the ability of the poorest families to pay. Some plead that they will pay later, and in the meantime take a loan from community funds; some will never be able to pay. This is ultimately recognized and their default is overlooked, a slightly heavier burden thus falling on the remaining households. But the *ad hoc* nature of this decision both delays the completion of the collection and encourages others to plead poverty. The poor who do pay their contribution deny themselves necessities: no meat is eaten, the children do not get new shoes; benefits such as a tarred road, though welcome, are to many a luxury which they would prefer to defer. Such feelings are more intense when the new service is seen as benefiting certain categories of persons more than others. (In some of the more thorough-going schemes of remodelling, the newly demarcated plots are allocated to those who can afford the overhead charges; an excess population, made up of those who are too poor to use such plots, are evicted; they carry their shacks and estera mats to a new site; yet, such remodelling is expected to be a community project in which all co-operate with equal enthusiasm.)

Graduated contributions, though desirable as a solution to some problems, would, however, be very difficult to assess. Incomes from informal sector activities are hard to calculate; and calculating per household, rather than per individual income, increases the difficulty. Sierra migrants tend to be secretive about money and many who eat well and educate their children live in relative material squalor, in poorly constructed and furnished homes. It seems equitable that those with good houses should pay more for comparable benefits – title, tarred streets, street-lighting etc. – but in the small community the differences between overt expenditure on housing and actual income are too well known (or suspected) to make this principle acceptable. And were a graduated assessment to be agreed, who would do the rating? The same constraints which deter men from disconnecting the electricity supply of a defaulting neighbour will also impede a rating exercise. Ties of kinship or godparenthood contradict the impartiality demanded. In particular, it is difficult to imagine the type of leader which the present system brings to the fore successfully engaging in such an exercise and winning the acceptance of rich and poor families in the community. Perhaps the answer lies in the imposition of a form of graduated assessment from outside the community. But the logical extension of this argument is that the pueblo should be fully incorporated into the municipality, its houses rated like those in its residential areas and services provided uniformly. However, the net flow of considerable funds towards the pueblo joven (rather than its obligation to improve itself from its own resources) is a principle which national and municipal governments have yet to accept.

When one examines the activities which the pobladores do organize, one finds that the above principle of equality does not operate. The fiestas or street-parties are, by general consent, successful. The overall organization rests with a very few people, usually the same people on each occasion; a larger number of women are involved in the preparation of food; again, the same people seem to be busy in a number of different contexts, and close ties of kinship or godparenthood between organizers and helpers are usually apparent.

Many pobladores participate in the fiesta but here they are able to spend according to their means and inclination. At the pachamanca, plates of food were sold at S/.100 (a day's minimum wage), and many families were seen to share a plate, while others bought only soft drinks. Such fiestas are, in fact, a means of taxing members of the community according to their capacity to pay (this also invites some of the men to spend more on beer than they would otherwise do). It is always hoped that the fiesta will attract visitors from outside the community, but the advertising is quite insufficient and the nature of the activity – usually a sapo tournament between the few committees – is not one which holds attraction for outsiders. The sums raised by these fiestas seem to range between S/.5,000 and S/.10,000, a commendable figure given the size and resources of the community, yet so minute in comparison with the sums needed for development that the organizers are apt to become discouraged.

(One might compare the manner in which the middle classes obtain services for their neighbourhoods to that which is expected from the poor. If a middle-class locality needs, for example, a kindergarten, a few people constitute a pressure group: these are usually housewives, retired persons or others with ample time; they have better resources such as telephones and cars; they are educated both in the literal sense and in understanding bureaucratic procedures; they have contacts as some of them will have close friends in the relevant offices; they collect signatures on a petition from their constituents, perhaps call a general meeting to advertise their demands; and they lobby the officials, and ultimately the municipality (or other agencies) provides the service demanded. In contrast, the poor are expected to engage with few resources in a similar level of activity and, furthermore, to involve both a number of participants in time-consuming activity and the entire community in the financing of the project.)

Community solidarity or mutual envy

The main concern of the pobladores of the pueblos jóvenes is to rise above their poverty. The older people realize that they will never be able to improve their qualifications though they may seek more stable employment; their hopes lie with their children. They wish to educate them and to provide them with such home conditions as will facilitate their learning. When their community can give them a primary school, water and electricity, they are relatively satisfied. Subsequent developments – notably those of the kind described in this chapter – do nothing to improve the employment situation and the possibilities of upward social mobility. People want to get out of slums, not merely ameliorate conditions within them. Little or nothing that is organized at the level of the community is likely to help them achieve these aspirations. Their resources are their own efforts, their social networks of close kin and paisanos. Individualism is a dominant theme.

Co-existing in Medalla Milagrosa with the expressions of community solidarity and loyalty is a deep sense of envy and status distinction. The one engenders the other. It is because all have such a similar migration experience – they left sierra villages for a corralón in Lima, they moved from there to Medalla Milagrosa, setting up their estera huts – that the subsequent success of some seems galling to others. Several of those who first built in mud or brick, or who now have the best houses, are the later arrivals to the community. Symptomatic of this envy is the relatively small degree of inter-family co-operation in Medalla Milagrosa, either in daily activities or in house-building; the restriction of children indoors rather than allowing them to play in the street; and the denigration by the wealthier of the poorer for their drunkenness, dirty habits and the like, in terms little different to those employed by residents of the neighbouring affluent housing estates for the pobladores of Medalla Milagrosa.

This individualism seems to take a number of forms, none of which can be clearly attributed to a defined social category, for personality differences ultimately intervene.

Among the well-to-do in Medalla Milagrosa there are some who could perhaps afford to move to a low-cost house in an urbanization; but the house would be smaller than their present one, and there would be the difficulty of selling the latter. In addition, they enjoy the comradeship in Medalla Milagrosa, so they stay, and continue to improve their house. For them the advantages of a legal title are balanced by problems threatened by remodelling, and their best tactic seems to be to push hard for neither title nor remodelling, and to hope that the quality of their house will suffice to leave them unaffected. As the social distance between them and their neighbours increases so does their life become focused upon the family; if the parents have high aspirations for their children, they will be more inclined to keep them indoors doing homework; if the parents are gregarious types, they will continue to participate in community activities.

Among some, whom one suspects of being downwardly mobile, individualism is even more vehemently expressed. One resident of Medalla Milagrosa still lives in a poorly furnished house even though he has a stable government job; he seems to have lacked promotion; he repeatedly refers to high officials with whom he has had close relationships. He describes vividly the way in which the poor are exploited, but attributes this to the workings of the social system; a system whose laws are not man-made and capable of change, but immutable. He holds that in such a situation all that one can do is to isolate oneself from one's kin, neighbours and community, and fight for oneself. (His wife, a leading member of the Club de Madres, does not share this desire for exclusion; but she is a very religious woman and cannot be drawn into any political discussion.) These people seem to put such pressure on their children that they become psychologically disturbed; one youth, however, has won a place in the best private university in Lima; his parents are paying part of his fees, which perhaps accounts for their material poverty. One such resident, though formerly an office-holder, still an influential man, and well integrated into the community through ties of kinship and god-parenthood, is described by the present leaders as one of the prime obstacles to communal activity.

The very poor, in contrast, contribute little to communal activity because they have nothing; their earnings are so low that they default in their contributions; so much of their time is spent looking for work, or in second occupations, that they cannot attend meetings or engage in communal tasks. Yet these people often do display an overt activity and concern for the community. They are more dependent upon the community for emotional support; they are more likely to experience such total destitution that the community will rally round to help them; their poor houses would probably be the first to be eradicated in an improvement scheme and they need the support of the leaders for protection. These people, in fact, may contribute a much higher proportion of their resources than other residents.

In the broad middle range, individualism and community affiliation are more evenly balanced. Some families seem to withdraw from communal participation, and having stronger aspirations to leave Medalla Milagrosa, put greater pressures on their children to succeed in school. In other families there is less interest in investment in schooling, and more in immediate consumption such as better furnishings. Some men are outgoing, enjoying the tasks and prestige of leadership. But all these families are trying to get ahead; some place more emphasis on hard work, others on a network of personal contacts which will provide opportunities, others on current consumption which raises their status amongst their neighbours. The improvements and services sought by the community offer nothing towards the realization of these aspirations.

In a community such as Medalla Milagrosa the differences in wealth derive from occupations located outside the settlement. A few traders make their profits from sales to neighbours, but the rewards are small; the women provide only a secondary income in their households. But as families grow and seek to add new rooms, as wealth enables them to contemplate better houses, a conflict arises between those with insufficient land or house-space and those who are well provided; for now in Medalla Milagrosa, there is no longer any vacant area into which the community can expand. But there seems to be no crystallization of these

have and have-not categories into groups or factions mobilized in articulation of their respective interests. First, too many ties of kinship, common origin and the like cut across these divisions. Secondly, the have-nots
are likely to perceive a solution to their problems through their individual
relationships with the 'haves'. And thirdly, as a small minority (and in the
case of tenants, lodgers, and married sons living at home, a minority
without a vote in community councils), the have-nots can influence the
reallocation of land, through a remodelling process, only through the
community.

In many ways Medalla Milagrosa appears, at first sight, a most atypical
pueblo joven. Its cliffside location has brought it into a more repeated and
intense confrontation with the surrounding landowners, the residents of
the new estates and the municipal authorities; yet, it is probable that this
has aided them in the acquisition of basic services, services which many
communities of a similar size do not enjoy. In few settlements would one
expect to find so striking a character as Señorita Yolanda Félix; yet in
many ways she is typical of the young person alienated from her community, by absence, education and experience, who tries to achieve reform
through aggression against the leaders rather than by gentle persuasion.
However, the factors suggested above which engender the low level of
communal activity in Medalla Milagrosa seem likely to be widely applicable in other small pueblos jóvenes.

The legally complex and lengthy bureaucratic procedures necessary for
attaining property titles and services, though common in all aspects of
administration in Peru, are immensely costly to the pobladores of a
pueblo joven who, in fact, have less time and money available than more
affluent citizens. (In Western Nigeria, for example, a house-owner could
obtain legal title to his property in a fraction of the time and cost that is
being imposed on the people of Medalla Milagrosa.) Again the government agencies, in insisting upon certain self-imposed technical standards
and in passing on to the consumer considerable overhead charges, fail to
provide new services as cheaply as might be possible. When this is
compounded with delays and perhaps with the repeated failure of applications, the pobladores grow frustrated and their efforts weaken; this
frustration from having tried is often not distinguished from the alleged
apathy of those who have not attempted to achieve the desired amenities.

In the apparent attempt to distribute widely the committee offices, the
regulations imposed by SINAMOS seem to have resulted in the assump-
tion of leadership by men and women who are keen and willing, but who
lacked the resources necessary for the successful fulfilment of the role. In
particular, whilst they might have been adequate in everyday administrative tasks, they had neither the time nor the influential contacts necessary
for the execution of development projects. Perhaps the SINAMOS offi-

cials saw themselves as occupying this role; in most cases they were, for one reason or another, ineffective.

In most older pueblos jóvenes one finds a range of wealth and success similar to that described for Medalla Milagrosa. The same problems are thus likely to occur in collecting equal contributions for services. This differentiation in wealth intensifies the individualism of the pobladores, already a dominant characteristic deriving both from their peasant origins and from their interpretation of the urban occupational scene. In other circumstances the very wealthy and the very poor would move out of the community into others which would reflect more accurately their social status; in the pueblo joven this tends to be difficult; people are trapped within the community. One subconscious means of resolving the tensions created by individualistic envy is to emphasize more strongly the loyalty to the solidarity of the community; this means is manifest in the regular fiestas, in ties of godparenthood and marriage. Yet these ties, in deterring the imposition of sanctions on defaulting members, in rendering more difficult the imposition of differential rates of contribution, are, in effect, dysfunctional to the development of the community. It would seem that one needs an external agent, not to raise the aspirations and consciousness of the pobladores, but to resolve the contradictions existing between individualism and communal solidarity.

In the larger pueblos jóvenes such difficulties are less likely to arise. Small local blocks may enjoy a sense of cohesion; they may organize their own fiestas; but they are part of a larger territorial unit. The leadership of this unit is much more divorced from the intricate network of interpersonal ties at the local level; it can act with greater impartiality; it commands much greater resources. It is, in fact, on the way to becoming a municipal authority; some of the larger and earlier pueblos jóvenes, San Martín de Porres and Comas for example, have already attained municipal self-government; here once again one begins to hear charges that the new municipal authorities are too remote from the mass of the people. At this level one is no longer talking of community development in the sense of mass popular participation that the term usually implies.

In the larger pueblos jóvenes, too, there are a higher number of wage employees having common economic interests; some of them will be active trade union leaders. Community councils become a forum for the articulation of political discontent; leaders see community office as a stepping-stone to a political career. The council of Villa el Salvador recently called upon the government to nationalize private banks and increase its control over multinational corporations, as well as generally increasing its support for social-property enterprises, establishing local newspapers, and reducing the prices for basic services such as water and electricity. One of Villa el Salvador's most prominent leaders – Señor

Aragón – became a nationally recognized radical politician; on occasions he has even been arrested with other militants.

The leaders of Medalla Milagrosa do not discuss political issues in their meetings; they focus upon communal needs and see that their achievement will be realized through patient collaboration and negotiation with government and its agencies, and with charitable bodies. Individually they tend to eschew political activity. In these circumstances – the inability of the community to act collectively in pursuit of its stated goals, and the apolitical attitude of the pobladores, leaders and masses alike – it seems unwise to expect that the small pueblos jóvenes will form a basis for successful social and political mobilization.

6. Marginality

Any description of a single pueblo joven such as Medalla Milagrosa tends to stress the initiative of its members: in founding the settlement, in building their houses, in finding jobs for themselves, and in gaining public services such as light, water and sewerage. They act with little apparent help from the state. And, thus, the autonomy of the settlement is emphasized. The social anthropologist, making his micro-study of the little community, tends to focus on those social processes most obviously located within the bounds of the community. But the pueblo joven has developed as it has because of the constraints set by the state in particular and society in general. People have been obliged to invade land and build their own houses because of the comparatively high cost of living in inner-city slums and corralones, because of eviction from such areas and because the so-called low-cost public housing is beyond their means. One task of the social anthropologist, acknowledged especially by those engaged in urban study, is to unite the micro- and macro-approaches, to set his study of processes within the community in the framework of those processes ongoing in the wider society, and to indicate the parameters within which the pobladores are able to operate. In looking at the small community one studies its responses to pressures and constraints imposed from without; and one also observes the impact which these responses have, in turn, on the world outside. Such an approach, moreover, is likely to produce generalizations valid for the majority of such settlements; comparison between settlements yields only an image of their considerable diversity.

In Latin American literature, the relationship between the state and the squatter settlement is subsumed in the concept of *marginalidad* – marginality. As I have already noted in the opening chapter, the term, so used, has not been widely employed outside this continent. It originated, probably, in the concept of the marginal man – the man caught between two cultures, and experiencing psychological tensions leading either to innovative behaviour or apathy – which was popular in American sociology in the 1950s. It seemed appropriate to Latin American situations in which the Indian migrant to the towns no longer seemed to belong to his traditional rural culture, but nor was he accepted into the western urban culture of the city. The Peruvian cholo appeared to be a perfect example of the marginal man. Subsequently the term has embraced an ever-

115

widening range of meanings as it has been adopted by the social science disciplines. As the dominant themes of sociology have changed, the focus in Latin America shifted from 'integration' in the 1950s and 1960s, to 'dependency' in the present decade. Marxists and non-Marxists alike have incorporated the term into their analytical frameworks. In popular usage the term has become a euphemism for 'the poor'; for most people it remains a pejorative term; but its mode of use does tend to indicate the particular viewpoint held by the user in accounting for poverty – thus the way in which the term is used tends to direct attention towards certain problems or issues rather than others. Diversity results from the transposition of the term into different parts of speech. It may be used as an adjective: *barrios marginales* – marginal settlements; as an abstract noun: *marginalidad* – marginality; as a collective noun: *los marginados* – the marginated (or marginalized); in a verbal form: *sin marginación* . . . – without the margination (or exclusion) of . . .

In this chapter I tackle two issues simultaneously: I want to explore the usefulness of marginality as a concept in aiding our understanding of the pueblo joven. In so doing I shall be indicating the relationship between the small settlement and the state. I shall focus upon Medalla Milagrosa. In many respects it is less marginal than other forms of slum settlements in Lima, such as the tugurio, corralón or the recent pueblo joven with most of its inhabitants still living in estera huts. Yet, because it is a designated pueblo joven, because of its location and the poverty of its people, it would certainly be regarded as marginal by those who are familiar with the term.

The concept defined

Marginality is, in essence, a spatial concept; but one may order space in different ways. In a single statistical continuum, the margins fall at either end. Thus, those with marginal incomes are those with the greatest and the least; normally, one would only regard those with the least incomes as marginal, for it seems unusual to designate the very rich as marginal. Again, one may describe two discrete, independent but juxtaposed categories, and describe as marginal those items which fall clearly into neither category. Thus the cholo is poised between rural Indian and urban western society, a foot in both but belonging to neither. Yet again, one may envisage a single category or system in which items are being pushed out of, or excluded from, the category or system; this process of exclusion contrasts with that of integration which is usually implied in the previous image. Here the excluded, however, may become a distinct category, or form their own system, so that the duality of the previous image is restored. Cardoso (1973) and Touraine (1976) have both argued that marginality is the consequence of contradictory processes of exclusion and integration: the former writes of the collapse of the traditional sector or economy and the failure of the modern economy to absorb its members; the latter more specifically refers to the discrepancy between the rate of rural emigration and the paucity of urban wage employment. In the following discussion of the usage of marginality, the salience of these different spatial and processural images will be apparent. In some contexts marginality denotes a situation, in others a process. Individual scholars have tended, however, to use the term not in any very limited sense, but in a range of contexts; sociologists such as Quijano have developed the usage of several of them over time. However, in this chapter I am concerned not to trace the development and consistency of these usages, but to apply them to a specific community; thus I shall rarely ascribe certain usages to particular writers.

In its statistical usage, marginality is widely used to refer both to places and to people. Squatter settlements are marginal in that they are located on the periphery of the city (the continuum here being between centre and periphery). Very many of the large pueblos jóvenes of Lima are indeed marginal in this sense, and a greater proportion of the pobladores live in these settlements rather than in those within the city's urban area. Medalla Milagrosa, like the many pueblos jóvenes in the industrial area between Lima and Callao, is not marginal in this sense. But settlements are also marginal in that they are sited on land which is deemed unfit for recognized housing developments. In this sense many of the large peripheral pueblos jóvenes are not marginal: they are located on flat or undulating land. Using this criterion, Medalla Milagrosa is certainly marginal: its houses, being built into the sides of the gully, are highly vulnerable to severe earthquakes. Marginal too are the settlements on the steep-sided slopes of El Agustino and San Cristóbal and those on the banks of the Rímac river. In every pueblo joven almost all the individual houses are marginal, as judged by standards employed by municipal authorities; the majority are clearly substandard and even the best houses would probably fail on some technicality.

People are statistically marginal in terms of the correlates of poverty. As we already know, those with the lowest incomes are marginal; and here income has to be set against the size of family. In a situation where wives are frequently earning and even young children may find some opportunity for petty remuneration, it is the household income which is significant. Those with irregular sources of income are also marginal: the wage earners employed by construction firms which hire labourers for a specific contract and lay them off upon its completion; or the self-employed artisans whose orders fluctuate according to season. Again, marginals are those without entitlement to social security and without

savings to cushion them against sickness and other such disasters, and
against income irregularity. Most of the pobladores of Medalla Milagrosa
are marginal in this sense.

In these statistical usages of the term marginality a number of variables
are used. And though many individuals may be marginal on all counts – in
that they live in substandard houses on unsuitable terrain in peripheral
settlements and have low and irregular incomes, no social security or
savings – it is clear that there are many who are marginal on some
variables but not on others. In Medalla Milagrosa there are a few families
who have a moderately high and regular income. Again, the criteria
adopted here embrace different proportions of the total population; the
use of housing standards or an officially recognized (but unrealistically
high) Poverty Datum Line results in well over half the total population
being classed as marginal. Ill-housed and poor they most certainly are;
but one feels that one needs a term to describe the bottom 10 per cent in
the society: the minority who fall at the margins of the continuum rather
than the majority who fail to meet middle-class living styles.

Dualist and integration theories

Dualist theories of society differ in the manner in which they define the
two dominant structures or systems; yet generally and descriptively the
dichotomies expressed are similar. On the one hand one has a modern,
western-oriented, urban white and capitalist society; on the other a
traditional, rural Indian and peasant society with its indigenous culture.
Each of these is seen as a largely autonomous structure, the former being
imposed from without, upon the indigenous society. However, the situation of contact is not a static one, for while the modern system is in the
process of growth, the traditional one is withering away. The movement
of people from one system to the other is thus a one-way process: from
traditional rural to modern urban structures and not the reverse. Those
people in mid-passage are the marginals, having left one structure (physically) but not yet incorporated (culturally) into the other. Two questions
are posed by this approach: how well are the migrants integrating into the
dominant structure, and are they doing so fast enough? Integration is
seen as a process involving considerable psychological strain, the effects
of which, at best, may impede the successful adaptation to urban life and,
at worst, create an urban population which is politically dangerous. With
the current rate of urban immigration, a slow process of integration
increases the size of this marginal population. Such themes predominate
in Quijano's early work on the cholo. In effect, he asks the same questions
as were being asked, in less academic terms, by the middle classes of
Lima. Will the cholos accept the values of the dominant group? Will they

constitute an apathetic mass? Will they *in extremis* create a new counter-culture (as for instance blacks in the United States have done) which threatens the dominant culture? In fact, Quijano saw the progressive modification of the culture of the lower-middle and urban-working class by the migrant intrusions, aided by the development of a nationalist ideology stressing populist themes and appealing more directly to the poor.

Integration is a loose and ill-defined term: broadly it encompasses the acceptance of the values of the dominant groups in the society and the participation in its institutions. Values here tend to be judged by behaviour: a broken home is a sign of a low respect for marriage; the observed elements of social disorganization, catalogued for instance in the concept of the culture of poverty, are taken as evidence for a rejection of the dominant values, and thus a rejection of the dominant culture.

Viewing the situation in this way, the middle classes, through their proliferation of aid-giving agencies, are concerned to help the poor migrant integrate. Vocational classes emphasize the middle-class way of doing things; social workers put individuals in touch with agencies which can provide help in particular predicaments. These attitudes and policies are embraced in the concept of *asistencialismo*, a term which is difficult to translate succinctly but which might be rendered as 'assistance-giving'. For those opposed to this practice the term is highly charged emotively. The work of the nuns in the Club de Madres of Medalla Milagrosa, and of the social workers who have been attached at various times to this community, falls clearly into this category of action.

Middle-class observers, looking from afar at the pueblo joven, are prone to stress the divergence between their own style of life and that of the poor; those who enter the pueblo joven stress how the pobladores are striving to enter the middle classes and share their life-styles. Mangin (1970, pp. xxxii–xxxiii) has asserted that the inhabitants of a squatter settlement are, culturally, much more like the middle classes of their own country than they are like the poor in other countries; he denies the universality of a subculture of poverty. But let us look specifically at the pobladores of Medalla Milagrosa, reiterating some of the descriptive points made in chapter 4.

Quechua is still spoken within some homes but all the pobladores (save some recently arrived elderly relatives) are quite fluent in Spanish; in some families parents are anxious that their children should not lose a fluency in Quechua, in others they seem unconcerned that the indigenous language might disappear. None questions the primacy of Spanish, and the official recognition given to Quechua by the government aroused little popular enthusiasm; at best, it made people less shy of publicly admitting their competence in this language. In dress also, the younger generation adopt purely western styles and the youths of the pueblo are indistinguishable from those of other types of community. Only the older people, and more especially the women, display Indian traits in their clothing and hair-styles. Sierra customs, such as the ceremonial cutting of a child's hair at the age of 3, are quickly falling into disuse.

As we have already seen, most of the families in Medalla Milagrosa are stable, and the elements of social disorganization – broken marriages, children distributed between foster homes and institutions – are relatively rare. The majority of the pobladores seem anxious to conform to those standards enumerated alike by middle classes and the church.

As so many writers have already stressed, the trauma thought to be experienced in migrating from a poor backward rural area to the noisy bustling city is, in fact, countered by the welcoming care bestowed by relatives upon the new arrival. He is housed and fed; he is helped to find work; he tends to be encapsulated within a community of people from his home area. We found in Medalla Milagrosa a number of cases of psychological illness, and of physical illness of suspected psychosomatic origin; but these seemed to be much more convincingly explained, not in terms of cultural adjustment to urban life, but either of poverty *per se*, of unhappy or unstable family life, or of an excessive desire to achieve. Examples of the last are provided by parents who are too demanding that their children do well in school, so producing psychological maladjustment in the children; there is also the particular instance of a young man from the pueblo who experienced a very intense and tragic love affair with a girl from the affluent neighbouring estate.

Perhaps the most poignant evidence of a desire to integrate into the dominant sectors of society is the intensity with which education is pursued. Parents want their children to go to secondary school and university though they may not know how to help them most effectively. Many send their children to primary schools outside the pueblo in order to enhance their chances of success. Those now passing through the universities see themselves as about to enter professional careers, enjoying the life-styles and privileges pertaining thereto.

One image of the urban poor presents them as living in a ghetto-like existence, isolated within their little communities and divorced from the wider urban society. It is probably true that many women and children living in peripheral pueblos jóvenes make infrequent visits to the city centre; but such would be true of people in outlying working-class suburbs in any city. The men tend to travel considerable distances to work because, save in the Callao area, pueblos jóvenes are not located very close to major areas of employment. The men and women of Medalla Milagrosa tend to work in the near-by suburban areas, but they often travel further afield to visit relatives. The headquarters of the Huancaray association is in Surquillo, a distance of approximately 9 kilometres. Lima's bus services, both private and publicly owned, are quick and cheap, a fare of S/.8 or S/.10 is charged irrespective of distance.

Knowledge of public matters is considerable. Many homes have a television set and programmes are watched by neighbours as well. Admittedly football matches and American soap operas are more popular than news bulletins; but the pervasive influence of the commercials, invariably showing white, middle-class persons, cannot be underestimated. Newspapers are regularly purchased and read. Lima's two 'quality' papers, *La Prensa* and *El Comercio*, cost very little more than the smaller tabloids, and thus one frequently finds the former in Medalla Milagrosa homes. In fact, in both quality papers and tabloids, sex and sensational stories associated with the cheaper western newspapers are conspicuously absent; the Lima papers are differentiated by their political approach and, in recent years with nationalization and a more uniform ideology, by a focus on the affairs of one occupational group: thus *La Prensa* is for the urban workers, *El Comercio* for the peasants, and the tabloid *Expresso* for the educators.

The people of Medalla Milagrosa share in urban services: they have light and water supplied by the national corporations, though their sewerage system is local. Their children attend state schools both within and without the settlement. Very little of the shopping is done in the pueblo and they go instead to the near-by municipal market of San Isidro, the more distant Surquillo market or the supermarkets in the affluent suburbs. When they fall ill they go either to the clinic in the parish headquarters or to one of the state hospitals. Few of the pobladores are regular church-goers, though almost all are nominal Catholics. The faithful attend the near-by parish church of the Virgen de la Medalla Milagrosa. Neither in Medalla Milagrosa nor in most pueblos jóvenes of Lima is there any strong adherence to evangelical protestant sects. A few pobladores have bank accounts but they tend not to seek credit either from banks or from building societies.

The pobladores identify the government in terms of its leaders. During the recent era of military rule the presidents have sought to be popular figureheads, and Velasco even more so than Morales Bermúdez. Few other military leaders have gained popularity; instead, notoriety for incompetence has been the fate of some. The multitude of organizations and offices, known by their initials, baffles the ordinary citizen. In the years prior to 1968 the pobladores voted in national elections; some of those in Medalla Milagrosa belonged to political parties and party allegiance was claimed in attempts to resist eviction.

The pobladores have no voice, however, in municipal government. But they are, as we have seen, very active in the affairs of their own community: a high proportion of them are office-holders, many more attend public meetings within the settlement and, on occasion, meetings in the SINAMOS offices.

If integration is defined as active participation, incorporating a belief that one has some impact on national affairs, then the pobladores of the pueblos jóvenes are realistic in seeing themselves as merely passive participants, recipients rather than instigators of policy. In lobbying SINAMOS officials they did not seek to change overall policy but merely to influence some minor bureaucratic decision in their favour. Yet, in stressing the pobladores' lack of power – exercised either through political parties or through trade unions – one wonders if their situation is not shared by the overwhelming majority of the population.

The migrant's continuing attachment to his rural home is frequently adduced as a mark of his failure to integrate into city life. If integration is defined as total commitment to the city, then an aspiration to retire to the village or to maintain one's farm as a form of economic security, represents a falling short of this ideal. Visits to one's home town or village are ambiguously construed; for does not the middle-class migrant also return to his provincial home to visit his parents? Much of the activity among persons sharing a common place of origin takes place within the city and is best interpreted as an adaptation to the insecurity of city life, even though these relationships do serve to reinforce ties with the home area. Encapsulation within the village community in the city serves to maintain adherence to peasant values and attitudes; but not all of these are incompatible with city life and some indeed – an orientation towards personal achievement, the capacity to organize collectively – are qualities which have seemed characteristic of the middle classes, in contrast to the apathy which is assumed to epitomize the lower classes.

Cultural marginality is now so discredited in most academic circles that to attack it further is to flog a dead horse; the concept is, however, still alive in much popular middle-class thinking. It has been discredited partly because integration is so difficult to define: at what point does the rural migrant become integrated? The objectively different behaviour observed by the middle-class person contrasts to the strong desire to share and participate in a middle-class way of life which is felt within the community. Furthermore, there is also little evidence of a high degree of apathy; the pobladores do not constitute a lumpenproletariat in the classic sense of that term: the lowest stratum of society which is either apathetic towards the dominant norms of society or else rejects them entirely, engaging in (what the dominant classes term) criminal activity. Nor is there any attempt to create a new counter-culture. As in so many similar countries, the attempts to revive traditional literature, music and dancing are largely confined to intellectuals, whilst the migrant poor immerse themselves in a westernized pop culture.

The conclusion, therefore, of an investigation along these lines is that the migrant poor are integrated inasmuch as they accept the dominant values in their society, and aspire to the life-style enjoyed by those wealthier than themselves. Their inability to reach the levels sought is a consequence of their poverty; failure to integrate – if one wishes to use such a term – is a result of the situation of poverty and not of the values or culture of the migrants.

The same dualist position is found in an economic context. The traditional indigenous peasant economy is contrasted to the modern capitalist economy of external provenance; both are seen as largely autonomous systems. Between these lies the informal sector of the urban economy: a sector dominated by very small enterprises, having simple technology and low output, organized on the basis of family relationships or those of clientage. Again, the view is expressed that the informal sector (along, too, with the traditional sector) will wither away, becoming incorporated within the modern sector. Until this event, it is marginal. But here as well, with the evidence of a rapidly growing informal sector, its continuing persistence is increasingly accepted and the question of its relationship with the dominant capitalist sector is being more fully explored.

The marginality of the informal sector takes several forms. It is said to contribute very little to the Gross National Product as a consequence of its low technology (and small output per worker), of the severe underemployment of men in this sector and of the high proportion engaged in tertiary or service (and hence non-producing) activities. To 'abolish' the sector would do no harm to the economic structure of the country. Against such a view it is argued that the production of the informal sector is both considerable *in toto* and vital in many aspects. Many of its activities are underenumerated: for instance, the value of the housing built by self-help methods in squatter settlements compares impressively with that of recognized housing built by public agencies and construction companies.

In a Marxist vein it is argued that the capitalist system requires a reserve army of labour – a body of men who alternate between wage employment and unemployment – in order to maintain wages at a low level. The magnitude or the surplus of urban immigrants over what is needed to constitute the reserve army is not functional to the maintenance of the capitalist system; the excess has no effect, for example, in further reducing wages.

The organization of the enterprises in the informal sector is held to approximate to a peasant mode of production rather than to that of the capitalist system; it is doomed to disappear with very few enterprises succeeding; their entrepreneurs would join the ranks of the petty bourgeoisie and the majority of workers would join the proletariat. For as soon as an informal sector business creates a profitable market for its product, a more highly organized capitalist firm with more advanced technology, will step in and manufacture the product at lower cost. But this process of the withering away of the urban informal sector, a marginal element consequent upon the introduction to the town of modes appropriate to the traditional economy, is denied by those who see the informal economy as a creation of the capitalist system, supporting its own ends. This viewpoint will be elaborated below.

If one looks at the occupations of the pobladores of Medalla Milagrosa, and they are similar to those of people in other pueblos jóvenes, one sees how clearly they are integrated into the dominant sector of the economy. Several people are actually engaged in manufacturing: some are in factories, others supply small boutiques and work at home. Several, too, are engaged in the construction industry, some working more or less regularly for big companies, others (often the older men) working on their own account. The gardeners and domestic servants are highly dependent upon the size and affluence of the new middle class (as they work in the modern formal sector) created by the recent capitalist economic development. Those who sell cooked food at work-sites provide a service to those of their own class at a low cost which enables wages to be kept down. None of the pobladores of Medalla Milagrosa is similarly engaged in providing cheap manufactured goods of low quality for the poor, though such trades are common elsewhere. The shopkeepers in the pueblo provide a service of convenience, rather than cheapness, for their neighbours. Lewis (1973) has estimated that only 15 per cent of the work force of the pueblos jóvenes are engaged in producing for or serving their own people.

In these circumstances the designation of the informal economy as marginal does not seem appropriate. Certainly one needs to examine the organization of enterprises within this sector, but even more necessary is the study of the intricate relationship between these enterprises and the ongoing processes in the dominant sector of the economy.

Finally, in reviewing both cultural and economic marginality, it will be seen that those who might, for one reason or another, be termed culturally marginal are not necessarily economically marginal. Thus factory workers, or those employed in the public services and earning a minimum wage, are not deemed to be economically marginal, but they will certainly have many characteristics of the culturally marginal, and by definition they are statistically marginal.

As Quijano and many others have stressed, and our own data amply illustrate, there is a considerable movement of persons, over a period of time, between formal and informal sector occupations: members of a family are engaged in each sector; some individuals work in both: a wage employee by day, a taxi-driver or seller of cooked food by night. There is, in fact, a stratum of people substantially homogeneous in terms of their migrant origin and city experiences who suffer greater poverty and insecurity than those in better wage employment or more established business enterprises. Thus Quijano has postulated a marginal proletariat and a marginal petty bourgeoisie located below the proletariat and petty bourgeoisie proper. There is a sense of cultural marginality here because those located at Quijano's marginal pole of society are not integrated, in contrast to those at the hegemonic pole.

Exclusion

Alternative to the dualist approach with its dichotomy between modern and traditional economic systems – the former advancing at the expense of the latter as the 'marginals' move from one to the other – is an approach which views the whole society as permeated by the new capitalist mode of production. Whereas in past decades capitalism was more concerned with the production of raw materials for western industry, today the developing nations of the Third World provide opportunities for profitable financial investment in manufacturing industry; the relatively high ratio of profits is consequent upon lower wage rates. As a result, highly capitalized industries are established, usually paying good wages (relative to local income structures) and maintaining favourable standards of employment, but providing relatively few jobs for manual workers. The middle class, employed both in such industries and in the public bureaucracies, increases in size providing a market for high-quality manufactured goods, some of which are made locally. The poverty of the poorer strata inhibits the creation of a sizeable market for cheap mass-produced goods.

In the rural area the impact of these changes is felt in improved health services which, in reducing mortality, cause a more rapid population increase. Modernization tendencies in the city foster land reform measures which do little or nothing to increase the number of persons working in agriculture. Faced with lack of opportunities in the rural area and the lure of employment in the city, the peasants emigrate. But the rate of emigration greatly exceeds the number of new jobs being created in the city. The balance is absorbed into the informal sector. Thus, as Webb (1977, p. 40) reports, the proportion of the total labour force of Peru employed in the modern sector rose from 18 per cent in 1950 to 21 per cent in 1966; but the proportion employed in the urban traditional sector as he terms it (the self-employed, domestics, those engaged in very small enterprises) rose from 24 per cent to 32 per cent.

As noted above, some writers have expressed this rural expulsion and lack of integration into the modern urban economy as a contradiction in the capitalist process; those not absorbed are the marginals. Others, however, see a single process which marginates or excludes men (the *marginados*). Older men are rejected when they can no longer compete with the young for heavy manual labour; young men are excluded in their failure to find wage employment.

The informal sector, into which these persons are pushed, is not independent of the modern sector. As Webb (1977, p. 69) writes, 'The best point of departure for a study of urban traditional sector incomes is the close relationship between this sector and the modern sector. First, the urban traditional sector has a high degree of trade dependency upon the modern sector: budget studies show that urban traditional sector families in Peru spend about half their income on food and about another quarter on factory goods or "modern" services such as medical and transport services. About three-quarters of their income is therefore spent on imports into the sector.' Furthermore, the two sectors are functionally related: low wages in the modern sector are possible because employees can obtain cheap services and goods from the informal sector, cooked food sold from stalls near their work-place for instance; they can rely on kin, both in town and in the rural area, for many elements of social security. In certain instances, the artisans working at home for the luxury boutiques reduce the costs of manufacture for the latter. Examples of all these modes of linkage have already been seen to exist in Medalla Milagrosa.

The informal sector – its people and their activities – is largely unregulated by the government. Minimum wage rates are not enforced, and many of the provisions of labour codes do not apply to small enterprises. Very few employers pay social security contributions, as required by law, for their domestic staff. Collectively the workers in the informal sector – the domestics, gardeners, petty traders etc. – have interests in common; but their relationship with the formal sector, the middle-class employers, is highly individualistic, and any possible cohesion is thus fragmented. Yet, it is of course the government which has the power to control their livelihood: in setting and enforcing minimum wages, in facilitating or impeding the issue of licences and other types of permits.

The use of the term *marginados* by radical writers implies not the pejorative tones of *marginales* but a feeling of scandal that men and women should be so impoverished. Some of the literature on Latin American shanty towns argues that the standards of living of the poor are steadily deteriorating. Thus Quigano writes: 'the working masses in general have been unable to prevent the constant reduction of their real wages and standard of living' (cited in Webb 1977, p. 43). However data supplied by Webb (1977) and Lewis (1973) do not support this gloomy picture, at least for the 1960s. The development of Medalla Milagrosa during this period is not an isolated phenomenon.

Webb (1977, p. 39) shows that in the period 1950–66 real income in the modern sector rose by an average of 4.1 per cent annually: wage earners benefiting more (4.9 per cent) than government employees (3.6 per cent); incomes in the urban traditional sector rose by an average of only 2 per cent: 2.5 per cent for wage earners and 1.9 per cent for the self-employed. Lewis (1977, p. 103) shows that between 1956 and 1969 incomes per household in the barriadas rose by 33.5 per cent, though with increasing family size the per capita increase was only 19.3 per cent. During this period the minimum wage was progressively increased: from 1970s it ranged around 5 per cent annually but began to rise sharply in 1973, reaching 24 per cent in 1975 and approaching 40 per cent in 1976. During this period the minimum wage was progressively increased; from a base line of 100 in 1968 its real value rose to 125 in 1972 and 122 in 1974; but it fell to 95 by the end of 1976. The effect of inflation, however, was felt more strongly by those earning 'average wages' and 'average salaries': their real incomes rose to 133 and then fell to 91 and 78. Yet for the very poor a sudden fall of 25 per cent in the real value of their incomes is very traumatic and the effects of this were clearly visible in Medalla Milagrosa in 1977, and were reflected in the apathy shown towards communal activity.

Whilst the majority of the poor have enjoyed improving living standards in the past two decades, they have not done as well as the more affluent. The proportion of income received by the poorest 40 per cent of the population fell in the period 1961–72, from 10 per cent to 9 per cent, whilst that of the wealthiest 5 per cent of the population rose from 26 per cent to 33 per cent. Webb's figures cited above illustrate the disparity between modern sector wages and informal sector incomes. Lewis' figures, comparing incomes of barriada residents with those in the rest of the city, show that the real incomes of the poorest 10 per cent of the population did not increase in the period described; he suggests that this basic minimum represents the level at which an immigrant can just support himself in the city, or the level which will attract him to the city; the two explanations are not contradictory.

Thus the poor, or most of them, have enjoyed rising standards of living in the last few years, until the most recent period of rapid inflation; but their incomes have not kept pace with those of wage earners who are either in good employment or strongly unionized, nor of the very rich. The disparity is the consequence of government policies. The Peruvian government emphasizes the development of major projects, facilitated by massive investment from abroad. Plans to expand the social property sector were widely publicized in the early 1970s but little was actually achieved before the scheme died in the changing economic climate of later years. Thus in 1975–7, enterprises with a total investment of S/.280 million were projected for Villa el Salvador with its population of a quarter of a million, but these were to employ only 1,100 persons. As Webb (1977, p. 83) describes, the burden of taxes in the 1970s fell as heavily on the poor as on the rich; during the 1960s the proportion paid by the poor doubled, though this increase did not continue through the 1970s. The communal labour used by the pobladores in developing their settlement is, in effect, a form of tax; for in the housing estates the services thus provided are paid for from state and municipal revenues.

The absence or non-implementation of social security systems for the poor has already been cited. The hospitals of Lima have been graded according to the social class of their clientele: employees and workers. Only in the field of education has there been no discrimination against the poor: thus Medalla Milagrosa has its primary school, even though half its residents prefer to educate the children elsewhere. As Webb (1977, p. 82) concludes, neither the liberal Belaúnde government nor the self-proclaimed revolutionary military regime of Velasco, did much to improve the lot of the poor; the policies of the present regime are likely to be even less effective. However the poor have benefited from a 'trickle down' effect from the increasing affluence of the strata above them. Webb (1977, p. 94) notes, however, that a 'selective transfer of 5% of the national income, taken from the richest 1% of the population and given to the poorest quartile, would reduce absolute income at the top by only 16% and would *double* incomes at the bottom'.

Government policies which determine income levels do not separate the population into clearly bounded groups of rich and poor; however, its housing policies do. An aerial view of Lima clearly shows widespread housing development of two types: the new middle-class estates and the peripheral pueblos jóvenes. In the former may be included the low-cost housing projects which, in effect, are available only to wage earners with regular employment; in the latter exist a very few pilot projects of cheap housing which have not developed further. The two areas are starkly distinguished: in the former the infrastructure – roads, water, electricity – is first provided, then the people move in; in the latter the people arrive first, and then struggle to obtain services. These two zones contrast with the third, the older urban area in varying stages of decay.

The pueblos jóvenes are, as Mangin emphasized, not a problem but a solution. For the pobladores they provide an opportunity to create their own housing instead of being subject to rising rents in inner-city slums and corralones as new waves of migrants seek accommodation. For the government they provide a solution in that the poor are housed at little public expense; public funds are channelled into housing for the middle strata; the poor are encouraged to save and pay for the installation of the services they require. In the late 1960s the construction of a motorway linking the city centre and the affluent suburbs absorbed half of the investment made by the municipal government of Lima; later the roads to the beaches continued to be the largest project.

Some of the larger and older pueblos jóvenes have already developed into independent municipalities; it has been the intention that Villa el Salvador should become a *ciudad autogestionara* – a self-governing city. But the small settlements which lie within the city, such as Medalla Milagrosa, in effect, are excluded from the municipalities in which they lie: they have no voice in municipal politics, pay no rates, and receive only minimal services (one result is that rubbish is collected from the entrance of Medalla Milagrosa). There seem to be no plans for their eventual incorporation which would mean a net flow of wealth towards the settlement, as richer areas would subsidize the poorer ones. If this happened, it would run counter to the main tenets of government policies towards the pueblos jóvenes, in that they should be largely self-financing.

As we have already seen there appears to be relatively little movement in or out of a once-established pueblo joven; the affluent who build good houses are both reluctant and unable to move to a low-cost housing estate; the very poor are not evicted. Two separate worlds are thus being created in Lima: one of housing estates graded by income; the other of squatter settlements; in both of these a great range of incomes exists. We appear to have come full circle; after arguing that the poor are not culturally marginal, that they have become integrated into city life, we reach a position in which the poor seem to live in a situation of apartheid.

Our bases of classification – income and residence – do not divide the poor in the same way. As many surveys (e.g. Lewis 1973; Gianella 1970) have indicated, the range of incomes in the pueblos jóvenes is not very different to that in other poor suburbs in the city; the pueblos jóvenes contain many who are in relatively good wage employment, though workers in the informal sector may predominate. The informal/urban traditional sector – modern/formal sector dichotomy divides people according to the mode of employment, but not according to income; for many employed in the latter receive only the minimum wage whilst some of those in the former have substantially higher incomes.

The pueblos jóvenes contain the poor of both sectors. Though they fall into different economic categories they tend to form a single social group due to the movement of persons between sectors, the shared life-styles and values. The marginated are those in the informal sector who, because of competition amongst themselves, receive low incomes, together with the poorer employees whose wages are low, substantially because of their relationship with the informal sector.

The concept of marginality is used by external observers to define the social position of the migrant poor, to account for their situation and to predict their future. It is not a term used by the poor themselves; I have not heard the people of Medalla Milagrosa describe themselves as marginal. How, then, do they see the society in which they live?

Political consciousness

In the early 1960s external observers tended to see the shanty towns as potential centres of revolutionary violence: urban riots in the USA fuelled such expectations; Fanon's theses on the role of the lumpenproletariat fitted them into a radical theoretical framework; the abject poverty and the focus on social disorganization – fostered by the popularity of Lewis' culture of poverty, and illustrated in Peru by Patch's description of a callejón (1961) in central Lima – made protest seem inevitable; the politically radical hoped for violence. The invasions of land by the squatters demonstrated that collective action by the poor was indeed possible. Yet when social anthropologists and others began to make a close study of the shanty towns, a very different picture emerged: one which stressed a substantial acceptance of the society with an emphasis on achievement. The invaders of land had become staunch defenders of their own property rights. In a sense, this position, too, was politically motivated by a desire to show that the poor were capable of and willing to improve their lot, and that the government should be encouraging them to help themselves, rather than letting them wait apathetically for the government to act. This approach, however, has detracted from the tension which undoubtedly exists among the poor. This tension was expressed, for example, in the widespread looting in February 1975 when police went on strike, in a march by tens of thousands of pobladores of Villa el Salvador which the police halted on the city outskirts, and in the sit-in in one of the big churches of central Lima by the women of a pueblo joven which was being eradicated by SINAMOS.

There would seem to be an incompatibility between the image of peaceful, achievement-oriented, law-abiding citizens of the pueblos jóvenes, aspiring for integration into the dominant sectors of society, and that of a population experiencing tension and frustration, hovering on the border of violence. The attitudes of the pobladores do, in fact, reflect their contradictory situation; they are clearly an integral part of the capitalist-urban structure, participating in it both in their economic activities and in assuming its values; yet they are excluded from its benefits inasmuch as their real standard of living, though rising for substantial periods, nevertheless increases more slowly than that of more affluent strata. The pobladores' view of the world embraces both an ego-oriented model which they use in the daily struggle for survival or improvement, and an externalized model in which they delineate the constraints to action. The former stresses achievement goals and patronage as a means of success. The latter views the society in class-like terms as they see the poor exploited and oppressed by the rich. These themes are elaborated below.

The images held by the poor should not be seen solely as the product of their own experiences – in growing up, perhaps in a rural area; in emigrating; in finding work within the town – but also as a reflection of, and response to, ideologies propagated by the government and dominant classes.

The present military regime has emphasized the revolutionary nature of its programme; the apparently more conservative economic policies now pursued are described as a 'consolidation of the revolution'. This government has, in fact, achieved much that previously elected politicians failed to do: in particular the programme of land reform by which the coastal sugar estates and the large haciendas have been transformed into co-operatives. The small peasant with his minifundio, however, has remained largely unaffected. Schemes giving employees a greater share in the ownership and control of the enterprises in which they work have been dropped. The military government has not done very much to change the overall policies and strategies which have provided so little housing for the poor.

The regime has argued that it seeks to build a society which is neither capitalist nor communist, but is one in which there is popular participation. Hence the stress on co-operative enterprises and workers' control of industry; and also on the high degree of popular participation expected in community councils. SINAMOS was charged with the mobilization of the people in these several directions. The mass of the people thus control their local residential and work situations; their influence on the state is problematic. The government sees the dialogue – in both public and private meetings – between the military leaders and the popular organizations as providing the link; a benevolent regime will respond to the demands of the people. In such a situation the class struggle becomes an anachronism. Populist policies, such as the legitimation of the Quechua language, reinforce the argument that the government is trying to provide for the interests of the poor; though as critics retort, its legislation brings them little or no relief from their poverty.

In stimulating popular demands, such an ideology obliges the government to be repressive, as these demands run counter to its own development plans. Financial resources are allocated to major industrial projects rather than to enterprises within the informal sector. SINAMOS, with less money available, became an agency for the control and repression of demands for services rather than for their stimulation. And as popular demands become more widely expressed, so must the government take a tougher line. In many ways the government would appear to be support-ing the political function of the 'myths of marginality' as outlined by Perlman (1976): to isolate the marginals from the organized working classes, to reinforce the idea that only with middle-class help can the poor achieve anything, to justify inequality and to shape the self-image of the poor.

The previous chapters have already described the individualism and achievement-orientation of the pobladores of Medalla Milagrosa; they do not seem to be atypical. Most of them enjoy in Lima a better style of life, in terms of material comforts, than that of their youth in the rural area. For the less successful, the example of others who have prospered provides a goal to which they may continue to aspire. In the informal sector, advancement is seen to depend on hard work and on the oppor-tunities provided by patrons. For the younger generation, education is the route to middle-class occupations and status. Not all families are equally ambitious; but the same qualities are needed by those who merely seek to hold their own. One may not aspire to a university education, but a completed primary schooling is essential if one is to qualify for any wage employment. Even the poorest must continue to struggle. But when extreme poverty is a consequence of bad luck, for instance a prolonged illness of a family member, depression and apathy frequently result; the individual feels that he can cope no longer.

In this ethos of individualism, lack of success is attributed to personal failings or to bad luck; for it is these which are most readily seen as the factors which differentiate between oneself and one's neighbour. The structure of the society which makes these factors so important is less often appreciated.

As writers see the marginality of the poor in terms of their exclusion from society, they are led to ask why they protest so little. A number of factors are adduced, and most of these seem as pertinent in Medalla Milagrosa as elsewhere.

The poor, in fact, are ignorant, though not in a pejorative sense. Their life experiences have given them very little understanding of the workings of government and its many agencies; the bureaucracy is seen as an almost impenetrable maze, and the man who can find a way through it is highly prized and admired. It is difficult for the poor to see how they are being exploited; in the large factory, the worker can see the levels of wages and profits as being related to each other; but in the informal sector the modes of exploitation are obscured by other ties: the apprentice does not see himself as exploited by his master for the latter will eventually train him and enable him to establish his own business. Many of those who describe themselves as 'self-employed' are in fact working for a larger firm: for instance, the tailor or shoemaker supplying a suburban boutique; but by designating themselves in this way they obscure their relationship with the capitalist system. Again, when men operate in different spheres – as wage earners by day and independent craftsmen or traders by night – and when family members are involved in productive relationships of different types, so is the development of any clearly formulated concept of exploitation impeded. Furthermore, the poor pay their taxes indirectly and hence remain largely ignorant of their contribution to government revenues. For the migrant, it is very difficult to envisage an alternative society except in the realm of fantasy. To subscribe to any specific policy of change implies an understanding, which is lacking here, of the existing system. Most people are able to distinguish their fantasies from their perceptions of the real world, though politicians may seek to stimulate the former in seeking popular support.

Whether self-employed in small establishments or in the more casual forms of wage employment, the worker is highly dependent upon the vertical relationship with patron or employer; it is on the manipulation of this relationship that his advancement or the retention of his job depends. Collective action with co-workers is likely to achieve very little. In the same manner, as we have already seen, collective needs, such as infrastructural services, are most successfully won by negotiation with the responsible government officials; one attempts to influence decisions made within a policy rather than change the policy itself. Portes (1972) has described the migrant as a guest in the town who feels that he ought to conform to the rules rather than change them; but his understanding of the rules may be so weak as to preclude the possibility of change.

It has been argued that migrants from a rural area where communal activity reached a high level (the Indian village with its councils and fiestas) would be more radical and better organized in the city than migrants from a latifundia (large estate) where landlord, and perhaps church, encouraged attitudes of extreme dependence. Migrants to Lima from sierra Indian communities do have an ability to organize, as the people of Huancaray illustrate, but their activity is directed towards the home community and not towards issues of urban poverty save in a most indirect way. Within the individual pueblo joven a relatively small number of persons is employed in firms with well-organized trade unions; others are in occupations in which potential union membership or activity is negated at the expense of ties of clientage with employer or foreman. For others, the gardeners or domestic servants for instance, no unions exist and the bases for common action seem very weak. In the bigger pueblos jóvenes, the aggregation of a large number of active trade unionists can result in the articulation of political demands at the community level: the demands of the Villa el Salvador council cited earlier are an example. But in the smaller settlements the active unionists are isolated and fragmented.

As we have seen, community solidarity can be strong in the smaller settlement. But the objectives of collective action are individualistic: one settlement is competing with another for services; organizations inviting the pueblos jóvenes in Lima for the purpose of making a common representation to the government have been short-lived and ineffectual, not least because of lack of official encouragement. When one settlement protests against delays in the provision of services or, in extreme cases, against eradication, its neighbours do not mobilize collectively on its behalf. Within the small community, differences between the interests of rich and poor pobladores are obscured by the many other ties which bind them: ties of kinship, common village origin and godparenthood. The ethos, engendered within such a settlement by its level and mode of collective action, serves to reinforce attitudes of individualism rather than class action among strata of the poor.

Modes of protest available to the poor are limited. Factory employees, organized in their unions, can bargain and strike in the normal manner. The self-employed may withdraw their services: for instance, taxi-drivers may refuse to operate; but whilst this causes some public inconvenience and draws attention to injustices, the hardship falls heaviest on the workers themselves. Such men, in addition, may organize a protest march but this does not have the coercive effect of a strike in an essential public service or major industry. Such protests are rather anonymously addressed to the 'government' rather than to any specific individual or agency; and, in any event, a change of personnel is unlikely to necessitate a change of policy. Unless the personnel against whom a protest might be directed are maintained in office, the goodwill already built up and seen as a necessary ingredient of goal achievement will be destroyed.

Finally, the pobladores of the pueblo joven may be mobilized by external agents. The urban poor can be a political force for they may be quickly mobilized. In many settlements in Lima university students have been active, but their efforts have been ephemeral and short-lived. In Medalla Milagrosa a group of students from the University of San Marcos, investigated the history of the community and dramatized it in a short play; but neither these nor any other students seem to have played a part in the community's struggles against eradication or efforts for services. The role of these young members of the community who are now university students is not, as was mentioned earlier, particularly effective. Nor does one often hear of such students playing a very active part in other settlements. The community leaders tend, as we have noted previously, to be conservative.

In the two decades before 1968 the major political parties made almost no attempt to attract a mass following in the barriadas; both presidents in office and presidential candidates have wooed the immigrant voter, as we have seen in chapter 3. They did so through general policies ostensibly aimed at alienating poverty, through an apparent toleration towards the creations of new barriadas, and through the support and assistance given in individual cases. From 1968 to 1977 political party activity was dormant, save for that of a few extreme left-wing organizations, strong among university students but little known in the pueblos jóvenes. SINAMOS rarely mobilized the pobladores of the pueblos jóvenes in mass demonstrations of presidential support as it did in the rural areas. Police repression also is an important factor in meeting overt opposition. Policemen are rarely seen within Medalla Milagrosa; however, the warning to the leaders that 'clandestine' evening meetings should not be held, indicates their vigilance. And when the poor do fall into police clutches extrication can be difficult; one Medalla Milagrosa youth spent over a week in custody after stealing some underwear belonging to the girl who jilted him. Stories are rife of the arrests of community leaders who are too vocal in their protests against the government or SINAMOS.

As one observes the day-to-day activities in a small pueblo joven such as Medalla Milagrosa, one sees little that might be termed political action, save for that directed towards community goals: participation in council meetings and lobbying visits to government offices. In contrast, house-building efforts and scholastic achievements are so apparent. It is thus understandable that progress and achievement should figure so largely in the reports of those who worked intensively within the community, whilst protest and class consciousness should dominate the writings of many of the armchair theorists who have rarely set foot within a shanty town. But there is also uncertainty about the definition of class consciousness; the position taken reflects one's own ideological stance. Define it widely, and class consciousness will be found within the pueblo joven; narrow the definition, and one begins to describe a variety of forms of political consciousness.

Several writers have described levels of class consciousness: an awareness of a separate identity – the recognition of common interests (that is, of a class nature, not ethnic or residential); the perception of these interests as being in conflict with those of other classes and the engagement in collective action to further one's interests; and the conception of class as determining the social order and change within it. In this progression one moves from the 'class-in-itself' to the 'class-for-itself'. It is clear that the pobladores of Medalla Milagrosa have achieved little more than a simple recognition of their own poverty – a poverty shared with those of other pueblos jóvenes and other types of slum. Their perceptions of their ethnic identity are considerably sharper.

It is argued, however, that one would not normally expect the situation in which the poor find themselves to generate a working-class consciousness of the higher levels; this is to be expected only of the political leadership. The followers engage in spontaneous action. Here the distinction is made between the consciousness which the poor have of the purposes and anticipated outcome of their action, and the real consequences of their action. Thus unstructured mob violence, possibly stimulated by a group seeking power, may lead to the collapse of a government unable to maintain order, and to its replacement by political rivals; but these may be either revolutionary or reactionary. However the mob is presumed to learn through its experience and to gain in political consciousness.

The demands made by the poor are essentially of a specific and short-term nature: trade unionists go on strike for higher wages, land is invaded to create a new squatter settlement and provide space for housing; the protest march focuses attention upon a grievance. In each case they seek to collaborate, in some way, with the existing powers in order to achieve their goals, rather than to confront them in such a manner as to substantially change the social order. The attainment of the higher levels of class consciousness necessitates that this qualitative distinction be bridged; but this is difficult, for activity of the former type serves only to reinforce the social order.

Allied with the debate about class consciousness is the relationship between the shanty-town poor and the working class or proletariat. The concept of marginality re-emerges here, not in the relationship between the poor and the dominant social groups, but between poor and proletariat. Are the poor culturally united with the proletariat? Will economic changes force more of them into the proletariat as only a few of the self-employed succeed in becoming established small entrepreneurs, whilst the majority are forced into wage employment? It seems unlikely that this postulated absorption will take place in the near future; as a category, the marginals will remain with us. In his own terminology Quijano emphasizes that the marginal proletariat and marginal petty bourgeoisie are only extensions of the major classes named; but, as he admits, the two marginal categories have so much in common socially: in their involvement in the informal economy, in their participation in the dominant economic structures through individual rather than collective relationships, and in their residence in small communities with strong cohesion (though these factors operate in various degrees); the marginals seem to constitute a social category distinct from the proletariat. The term lumpenproletariat is clearly inapplicable for them, if a rejection of the dominant values of the society is assumed by this term.

So one reaches the point of creating a category of persons socially distinct from the working class or proletariat and petty bourgeoisie or small entrepreneurs. For those who see this as a transitional category – either people pass briefly through it, and/or it will soon disappear – its apparent heterogeneity is of little interest. For those who see the marginals as persisting, a more positive approach is needed; for them the heterogeneity and fragmented nature of the category – one can hardly say class – is one of its prime characteristics.

In distinguishing between marginals and proletariat one is obliged to define a relationship between them. In Africanist literature a labour aristocracy has been portrayed, which uses its superior bargaining power to exact wage increases much greater than those enjoyed by the mass of the poor, and which has a vested interest in maintaining the modern capitalist industrial sector. Peruvian data, too, show that the organized workers in the modern sector have improved their real wages at a greater rate than workers in the informal or urban traditional sector. In pursuing their own claims, the unionized workers appear selfishly oblivious to the plight of the mass of the poor. A relationship of antagonism is thus assumed to exist; and in a slightly different context, as Perlman (1976) indicates, the very differentiation of proletariat and marginals is held to divide the working-class movement. Yet as other writers have shown, the 'trickle down effect' of wage increases benefits the poor too; as the more affluent wage earners receive more, so do they pay more for goods and services rendered by the marginals. The self-employed, domestics and the like raise their prices in accord with minimum wage levels. The poor thus support the organized workers in their demands. In a one-day general strike in Lima in July 1977, organized by the trade union federations, those in the informal sector obeyed the call and stopped work. This almost certainly indicated their sympathy with the very generalized grievance expressed against the government's handling of the economic crises.

The relationship between marginals and proletariat exists also in the social sphere. They are likely to share common rural origins and to be bound by many ties of reciprocal mutual aid.

It seems profitable, therefore, to distinguish between proletariat and marginals as categories which are qualitatively different yet related by ties of interdependence; superficially at least, this is not an antagonistic relationship. (The ultimate consequences of various possible government policies, for instance to base development on large-scale foreign investment in major projects or to stimulate small-scale artisan production, is problematic.) It seems likely that, in the immediate future, the informal sector will persist as migration to the city continues to outstrip the creation of jobs in the formal sector. Whilst many pueblos jóvenes improve, new accretions will be added and, perhaps, new settlements founded. The categories which have been described will thus persist in time. But will there be a movement of people through the categories as individual migrants, marginals on arrival, then enter the proletariat as stable wage earners, whilst others move in the reverse order? Evidence from Medalla Milagrosa shows how families become trapped within the pueblo joven: the rich cannot move out, the poor are not pushed out. Some capital accumulation is possible; but there are high risks that savings will be eroded and completely lost through sickness, unemployment or legal troubles. Yet some inter-generational mobility seems likely, as the successful university graduates find professional employment and live in modern housing estates. But the distinction between such estates and the pueblos jóvenes will maintain a sharp dichotomy in the urban society, only slowly to be occluded as some larger settlements develop, attain municipal status and approximate in character to the poorer urbanizations.

In suggesting that the marginals form a distinct category in urban society, one is of course confusing economic, social and cultural criteria. As noted above, not all residents of a pueblo joven are economically marginal: some are proletarians, wage earners in large modern enterprises. Yet if the definition is broadened to embrace persons with any traits of marginality, one is describing well over half the population. As the definition is narrowed, it would include marginal occupations or settlements, but rarely marginal people. But in the pueblo joven such as Medalla Milagrosa, and one suspects in many other similar settlements, one finds a mode of life determined in part by the economic relationships of the people, in part by the residential situation. To ignore either the latter relationship (as would many Marxists) or the former (as would some social anthropologists) would create a most misleading and inaccurate picture. In uniting them one is enabled to distinguish these settlements from other equally prominent forms of urban slum which in Lima are the tugurios, the callejones and the corralones. This has been our task.

7. Conclusion

Peru, in common with almost all developing Third World countries, has experienced a massive internal migration into the cities in the past two decades. This migration has completely outpaced the creation of new employment opportunities. The migrants themselves, in their poverty, have found accommodation in the extensive shanty towns which now characterize these cities.

In Peru the capacity of the rural area to absorb an increasing population has been very limited. A few areas of the selva are being opened up for commercial agriculture, but the sierra, where most of the population lives, contains almost no hitherto unused land. Nor have agricultural techniques greatly changed. The development of some of the haciendas in the middle of this century, and their subsequent expropriation in the land reform process, has not provided greater employment. The growth of the urban economy has been most marked in the manufacturing sector, with the development of highly capitalized industry; and in the service sector, with the creation of immense bureaucratic structures. These sectors have contributed to the growth of relatively affluent new middle strata whose life-styles contrast so strikingly to the poverty of those who have been unable to find wage employment, save perhaps that which provides minimal income and security.

The proportion of the Peruvian population now living in urban centres is high, relative to that of most African or Asian countries, indicating the more advanced level of economic development. It is, however, well short of the figure attained by some Latin American states – Argentina or Chile, for instance – though similar to that of many others. A striking feature is the primacy of Lima, which now contains a quarter of the country's inhabitants. The provincial towns and mining centres, for a variety of reasons – remoteness, lack of communications with a major port, absence of a local market – have failed to develop to any but a minimal degree. Nevertheless, some of these now have their own shanty towns, peopled by migrants from their own hinterlands. The processes of migration into these secondary centres are substantially similar to that into Lima.

The Peruvian government has done almost nothing to provide low-cost housing for the immigrant poor; nor has the private enterprise of the established middle strata. Very few poor sierra migrants have been able

139

to accumulate sufficient capital to build homes for the later arrivals. Vast new estates of homes for the relatively prosperous have been constructed since 1960, but their previous homes in the city have a high market value and are taken in turn by others of similar status. Much property in the inner city has degenerated into slum tenements, but the stock of such housing is being continually depleted as areas are redeveloped for prestigious and highly remunerative commercial and office building.

The barriadas, though seen by the administrator or planner as a 'problem', are a 'solution' to the urban poor. Their creation owes much to the desert environment of Lima which has provided large areas of level or undulating land suitable for building, and to the tolerance of the governments of the invasions of this land. In the 1960s the pueblos jóvenes, as they came to be designated, were given legal recognition, and their inhabitants were encouraged to develop their settlements from their own resources.

Many residents indeed, in the space of a decade or two, have succeeded in building modest houses which, though probably not conforming to established building regulations, do provide adequate shelter and comfort. It is thus assumed that policies stimulating self-help will result in the integration of the pueblos jóvenes into the city as working-class suburbs. But an alternative outcome seems possible: that, notwithstanding some development within the pueblos jóvenes, there will be little movement in or out of these settlements, and the urban population of Lima will be starkly divided between the pobladores of the pueblos jóvenes and the middle classes of the affluent estates.

By examining the processes which have led to the creation and maintenance of one small pueblo joven, I am led to conclude that the latter outcome is more likely.

Medalla Milagrosa is not a typical Limanean slum: the poor of that city live in a great variety of poverty-stricken settlements. Yet, in the manner in which its inhabitants have migrated to the city from the rural hinterland, settling first in inner-city tenements or corralones, and finding unskilled wage employment or working in the informal sector, Medalla Milagrosa is certainly representative of a larger universe.

Too few studies of individual communities have yet been made, but Medalla Milagrosa probably shares many features common to the smaller pueblos jóvenes. In particular, where these have been formed through relatively slow accretion rather than by mass invasion, the interpersonal ties between residents are likely to be strong, as newcomers have gained entry through introduction by existing residents. The defence of the settlement against eradication and the struggle to obtain essential services provides an initial focus for collective action. Strong loyalties to the community may be developed. Yet, as Uzzell (1972) has shown, the character of these communities can vary widely: in their initial attraction of more upwardly or downwardly mobile immigrants, and in their subsequent success or failure in establishing themselves, these settlements are ranged along the continuum from slums of hope to slums of despair.

The larger peripheral pueblos jóvenes contain a much higher proportion of the squatter-settlers, and their character differs markedly in many respects from that of the smaller communities. The higher levels of community organization become much more impersonal; these, in fact, may develop into a form of municipal government similar to that which has been attained in San Martín de Porres and Comas. Here one begins to hear familiar allegations that the leadership is growing remote from the mass of the residents. The aggregation of larger numbers of people with similar economic interests can result in the expression of demands in community councils properly relating to the work situation; thus, as we have seen, the council of Villa el Salvador, at times, has been highly politicized. In the larger pueblos jóvenes, costly plans to introduce new services or to remodel the settlement are undertaken on the initiative of richer residents and government agencies. Poorer residents who cannot afford the fees demanded, or who seem unlikely to be able to build a permanent house on the lot allocated, are evicted to the less desirable margins of the settlement. The large pueblos jóvenes are, however, divided into smaller units and wards, and though these are not identifiable on the ground by the casual visitor, these residents, like those of the smaller independent pueblo joven, have a sense of their own identity: they have their own governing council; they compete with neighbouring areas for services and development. It is possible that the process of land allocation has resulted in friends and kin living near-by; the original invaders were probably well known to one another and may have been able to reserve plots for a wider circle of their acquaintances. Yet interaction between residents of a small ward is not so firmly confined within its boundaries as in the case of Medalla Milagrosa.

The pueblos jóvenes contrast with other forms of Peruvian slum: the tugurios – the inner-city slum tenement or decaying mansion; the callejón – the purpose-built unit of rooms along a narrow alley; and the corralón – the collection of hovels on a vacant lot. In each of these settlements neighbours may share common rural origins as established residents notify newly arrived kin of vacant rooms. In many cases, there has been little movement in or out, and many residents have lived in the same buildings for a decade or more (Patch 1961). Such accommodation provides advantages such as its proximity to places of work, an important factor for the newly arrived migrant seeking a foothold in the city, but obliged to take casual employment in the initial weeks or months. But in these settlements accommodation is rented; and the threat of eviction is ever present as landlords decide to develop their individual plots, or as municipalities clear vast slum areas for more remunerative urban developments. Whilst co-residents may band together on occasion against an avaricious landlord, there is usually no permanent form of organization in these settlements. Residents have neither the right nor the desire to improve their property; there is little or nothing for them to defend.

The squatters of the newly founded pueblo joven are drawn from such inner-city slums; they have usually lived in the city for a considerable number of years. There is little or no evidence of substantial movement in the reverse direction. A planned move to a pueblo joven is made by those who have established occupations in the city, and who seek to invest in houses of their own the sums currently being paid as rent (the move may, however, necessitate higher travel costs). Fear of eviction precipitates such a move. But there are others evicted who do not enjoy such stability; they might prefer alternative accommodation of a similar character yet this is very scarce; they are forced into the pueblos jóvenes.

The pueblos jóvenes thus contain, at their inception, people whose wealth and security ranges widely; they are not merely creaming off the more successful migrants but also providing homes for the destitute. These initial differences, less overtly manifest when everyone lives in an estera hut, become magnified as the successful continue to prosper, and the poor struggle on without improvement: the former build good houses, the latter continue to occupy shanties, the estera mats replaced only by slightly more durable waste-materials. Yet neither rich nor poor are likely to move out: the rich because their houses have little market value and lack title deeds; the poor because in no other location would they be able to live more cheaply.

Only in particular situations, cited above, does a resorting of the population by wealth take place. However, differences in economic status cut across ties of kinship, affinity, co-godparenthood, and the like. Residents, in varying manners and in different degrees, participate in community organizations, focused upon their residential interests. For the majority, being either self-employed and lacking an association related to their occupation, or irregularly employed and only weakly attached to a trade union, the community council is the one forum where they may articulate demands; it is also through their community that their relationship with government is most apparent. Whilst their energies in finding jobs and in establishing little businesses are individually oriented, the community council provides the only opportunity for urban-oriented collective action (the activity of the village clubs is, of course, largely directed towards the village).

Descriptions of the pueblos jóvenes focus on the invasion of land, the residents' attempts to safeguard their illegally acquired squatters' rights, their individual activity in house-building and collective action in obtaining services. The emphasis is upon their achievement. But this must be seen in the context of government policy which both makes such achievement possible and, indeed, facilitates few other solutions to the migrant's housing problem.

Almost no low-cost housing has been provided in Lima in recent decades, either by government or by other public bodies, or on a smaller scale by middle-class private enterprise. Instead vast, new urban estates have been developed for the wealthier strata by huge companies, often multinationals, in which are allied the Limanean landowners, the construction firms, the building societies and such financiers. Promises of rent control have ultimately protected the landlords. Areas of slum housing adjacent to the city centre have been flattened to provide sites for prestige development: the Sheraton Hotel and Civic Centre complex, for example. Nothing positive has been done to stem the cityward flow of migration; toleration of squatting and periodic encouragement of public-works construction have at times provided incentives to the migrant.

In effect, for the past three decades the Peruvian government has tolerated land invasion and squatting. It has been accepted that eradication, though practised in a few cases, is no answer to a perceived problem, for the migrants merely decamp elsewhere. Furthermore, successive political leaders have sought, in a paternalistic manner, to woo the migrants into realizing the importance of their votes. In the past two decades the squatter settlements have gained legal recognition, first designated as barrios marginales, then as pueblos jóvenes. Initial hopes in the 1960s that the development of new settlements would be halted were unfounded, though latterly, with Villa el Salvador acting as a reception area for those evicted from other areas, the creation of new pueblos jóvenes does seem to have ceased. In authorizing the growth of these settlements on suitable terrain, the government thereby controls development. With the establishment of ONDEPJOV and then SINAMOS, services were provided through a single co-ordinating agency. The settlements were thus directly linked to higher organs of the state rather than to the existing municipalities or to individual public corporations. Though in the early years of the post-1968 military junta, the army was active in providing highways to facilitate access from the distant pueblos jóvenes to the city centre, now most of the development is to be paid for by the residents themselves; ability to make an initial contribution is rewarded by a loan either from the state or, in some cases, from an international agency. To achieve such development, community organization has been fostered from above, though the councils thus constituted have either replicated or replaced earlier committees. The forms of communal activity in Andean villages are cited as evidence of the migrants' ability to perceive the value of such activity. The mobilization of the population in small local units is stressed as a mode of self-determination and expression, and is seen, covertly, as a deterrent to class-based action. Thus SINAMOS, through its departments concerned with the pueblos jóvenes, existed both to channel locally generated activity towards development objectives and to control the expression of political opinion.

The interaction between government policies and the migrants' attempts to solve their housing predicament has resulted in the pueblos jóvenes (the form of squatter settlement particular to Peru, though sharing similarities with other Latin American squatter settlements). In Lima, and to a lesser extent in other Peruvian cities, contemporary housing development falls sharply into two categories: the pueblo joven and the middle-class urban estate. The poor live in the former, the moderately well-off to the very wealthy in the latter. But the division is not only between levels of wealth but also in the character of the two forms of settlement. In the middle-class estates, houses can be readily bought or sold; people can move as they prosper or fail, as their families increase or decrease in size. Little community activity exists; few social ties exist between neighbours. These are suburban estates typical of almost any city.

In contrast, the pueblo joven has many of the characteristics of a village community – though just how many is a matter for empirical study and not for assertion. The development of interpersonal bonds, the stability of residence, and the ability of its residents to organize themselves in defence of their property interests, all contribute to the belief that policies of self-help and communal activity will succeed in alleviating the poverty and misery of the pobladores. As we have seen, this seems unlikely; it ignores both the difference of interests between rich and poor residents and the manner in which personal ties can vitiate the imposition of sanctions and the consequent achievement of goals. But such policies of community development are successful in dividing the poor into small units competing with each other, in focusing energies on problems of the residential area rather than of the employment situation. The ethic of the informal economy tends to influence all sections of the poor; the failure to achieve community goals dampens enthusiasm and is expressed more in terms of the failures of the individual settlement than of the inadequacy of government policies.

The dichotomy between the two zones seems unlikely to be resolved in the near future. The existing residents of pueblos jóvenes are unlikely to move in any significant numbers into the housing estates, though the more successful of their children, in getting a university education and a professional career, may well do so. The larger settlements will continue, presumably, to develop towards a more independent municipal status, but as they do so the consequences of the difference in wealth amongst the pobladores will become more apparent.

Bibliography

The bibliography below contains a fairly comprehensive list of published works on the pueblos jóvenes of Peru; almost all, in fact, refer to those of Lima. Many of them have not been specifically cited in my text. The list, however, is not exhaustive and in particular it omits reference to a vast literature on housing (most of it consisting of official publications), and to the many theses, usually for the Bachelor's degree, which are held in Peruvian university libraries. The latter, though often theoretically and methodologically weak, do often contain valuable information.

Some authors have published similar material in a number of articles or books; I have tended to cite here those works which seem most readily accessible.

In addition to works dealing specifically with the pueblos jóvenes, the bibliography contains books providing a background to Peru's history and to contemporary social and economic conditions. For the reader's convenience I note briefly the following works: good introductions to Peruvian history are provided by Dobyns and Doughty (1976), Marrett (1969), Owens (1963) and Pike (1967). Despite the particularistic title, Sarfati Larson and Eisen Bergman (1969) provide a very wide ranging summary of political economic and social data of the late 1960s. The Peruvian economy is described by Thorp and Bertram (1978) and for the more recent period only by Fitzgerald (1979); Webb (1977) focuses upon income distribution. Bourricaud's monograph (1970) provides a picture of the political scene in the mid-1960s, while the symposia of Chaplin (1976), Lowenthal (1975) and Phillip (1978) describe the events and policies of the post-1968 military government. The growth of Lima is graphically presented by Deler (1975). Books giving a general overview of the pueblos jóvenes are few, but two books by political scientists describe the relationship between the settlements and the government: Collier (1976) focuses upon policies; Dietz (1979) provides a more detailed description of the relationships between government agencies and the pueblos jóvenes. Matos Mar (1966) has produced good surveys of the 1950s and Gianella's survey (1970) gives the most reliable data for a later decade.

The bibliography includes of course other works, not concerned with Peru, which for comparative purposes have been cited in the text.

146

Aduriz, J. 1969. *Así viven y así nacen*. Lima: Cuadernos DESCO A3.

Aguirre Gamio, Hernando. 1974. *El Proceso Peruano*. Mexico City: Ed. El Caballito.

Alcocer, F. 1954. 'La vivienda en Lima: problema y solución', *Latinoamericana*, 6:65.

Alderson-Smith, G. 1975. 'The social basis of peasant political activity', D.Phil. Thesis, University of Sussex.

Alers, J. O., & Applebaum, R. P. 1968. 'La migración en el Perú: un inventario de proposiciones', *Estudios de Población y Desarrollo*, 4:2.

Altamirano, T. 1977. 'Las relaciones urbano-rurales a través de las asociaciones regionales en Lima', Doctoral Thesis, University of San Marcos, Lima.

Andrade, G. A. 1963. *Estudios de Barriadas*. Lima: Instituto de Planeamiento de Lima.

Andrews, F. M., & Phillips, G. W. 1970. 'The Squatters of Lima: who they are and what they want', *Journal of Developing Areas*, 4:2.

Anon. 1970. 'Previ: Lima low cost housing project', *Architectural Design*, 40.

Austin, A. G., & Lewis, S. 1970. *Urban Government for Metropolitan Lima*. New York: Praeger.

Berckholtz Salinas, P. 1963. *Barrios Marginales, Aberación Social*. Lima.

Bishop, M. E. 1970. 'Political information seeking in the mass media, political knowledge and democratic orientation in Lima, Peru', Ph.D. Thesis, University of Wisconsin.

—— 1973. 'Media use and democratic political orientation in Lima, Peru', *Journalism Quarterly*, 50:1.

Boggio, K. 1970. *Estudio del Ciclo vital en Pamplona Alta*. Lima: Cuadernos DESCO A6.

Bonilla, F. 1973. *Pueblos Jóvenes y Urbanizaciones Populares*. Lima: Ed. Mercurio.

Bourricaud, F. 1964. 'Lima en la vida política peruana', *America Latina*, 7:4.

—— 1970. *Power and Society in Contemporary Peru*. London: Faber.

Bradfield, S. 1965. 'Some occupational aspects of migration', *Economic Development and Cultural Change*, 14:1.

—— 1973. 'Selectivity in rural–urban migration: the case of Huaylas Peru', in *Urban Anthropology*, ed. A. Southall. New York: Oxford University Press.

Brett, S. 1974. 'Low income urban settlements in Latin America: the Turner Model', in *Sociology & Development*, eds. E. de Kadt & G. Williams. London: Tavistock Publications.

Bromley, J., & Barbagelata, J. 1945. *Evolución urbana de la ciudad de Lima*. Lima: Concejo Provincial de Lima.

Caminos, H., Turner, J. F. C., & Steffian, J. A. 1969. *Urban Dwelling Environments: an elementary survey of settlements for the study of design determinants*. M.I.T. Report 16. Cambridge, Mass.: M.I.T. Press.

Caravedo, B. *et al.* 1963. *Estudios de Psiquiatría Social en el Perú*. Lima: Ed. del Sol.

Cardoso, F. H. 1973. *Estado y Sociedad en America-Latina*. Buenos Aires: Neuva Visión.

Castillo Rios, C. 1974. *Los niños del Perú: clases sociales, ideología y política*. Lima: Ed. Realidad Nacional.

Castro, A. 1965. *Diagnóstico de Barriadas en Lima*. Lima: Oficina de Planificación, Sector de Vivienda y Equipamiento Urbano.

Chaplin, D. 1967. 'Industrialization and the distribution of wealth in Peru', *Studies in Comparative International Development*, 3:3.
—— 1970. 'Industrialization and Labour in Peru', in *City and Country in the Third World*, ed. A. J. Field. Cambridge, Mass. : Schenkman.
Chaplin, D. (ed.) 1976. *Peruvian Nationalism: a Corporatist Revolution*. New Brunswick, N. J.: Transaction.
Cole, J. P. 1956. 'Some town planning problems in Greater Lima', *Town Planning Review* (Liverpool), 26.
Collier, D. 1971. 'Squatter Settlement Formation and the Politics of Cooptation in Peru', Ph.D. Thesis, University of Chicago.
—— 1971–2. 'Política y creación de pueblos jóvenes en Lima', *Estudios Andinos*, 2.
—— 1973. 'Los pueblos jóvenes y la adaptación de los migrantes al ambiente urbano Limeno', *Estudios Andinos*, 3:3.
—— 1975a. 'Squatter settlements and policy innovation in Peru', in *The Peruvian Experiment: Continuity & Change Under Military Rule*, ed. A. F. Lowenthal. Princeton, N. J.: Princeton University Press.
—— 1975b. 'Politics of squatter settlement in Peru', in *Peruvian Nationalism: a Corporatist Revolution*, ed. D. Chaplin. New Brunswick, N. J.: Transaction.
—— 1976. *Squatters and Oligarchs: Authoritarian rule and policy change in Peru*. Baltimore: Johns Hopkins University Press.
Cornelius, W. 1975. *Politics and the Migrant Poor in Mexico*. Stanford, California: Stanford University Press.
Cornelius, W., & Dietz, H. A. 1974. 'Urbanization, demand making and political system overload: political participation among the migrant poor in Latin American cities', *American Political Science Review*, 68.
Cotler, J. 1967. *Estructura social y Urbanización*. Lima: Instituto de Estudios Peruanos.
—— 1970. 'The mechanics of internal domination and change in Peru', in *Masses in Latin America*, ed. I. L. Horowitz. New York: Oxford University Press.
Cotler, J., & Laquian, A. A. 1971. 'Lima', in *Rural Urban Migrants and Metropolitan Development*, ed. A. A. Laquian. Toronto: Intermet.
Deler, J. P. 1975. *Lima 1940–1970: Aspectos del crecimiento de la Capital Peruana*. Lima: Centro de Investigaciones Geográficas.
Delgado, C. 1967. *Notas sobre Movilidad en el Perú*. Documentos teóricos, 6. Lima: Instituto de Estudios Peruanos.
—— 1969. 'An analysis of "arribismo" in Peru', *Human Organization*, 28:2.
—— 1969. 'Three proposals regarding accelerated urbanization problems in metropolitan areas: the Lima case', *American Behavioural Scientist*, 12:5.
—— *Problemas Sociales en el Perú Contemporáneo*. Lima: Instituto de Estudios Peruanos.
Dietz, A. G. H. 1969. 'Urban squatter settlement in Peru; a case history and analysis', *Journal of Inter-American Studies*, 11:3.
Dietz, H. A. 1974. 'Becoming a poblador: political adjustment to the Lima urban environment', Ph.D. Thesis, Stanford University.
—— 1976. *Who, How, and Why: Rural migration to Lima*, Center for International Studies, Migration and Development Study Group. Cambridge, Mass.: M.I.T. Press.
—— 1977. 'Land invasion and consolidation: a study of working poor/governmental relations in Lima, Peru', *Urban Anthropology*, 6:4.
—— 1977a. 'Some local-level structural determinants of differential participation among migrants', in *The Impact of Rural Urban Migration*, ed. J. White. Chapel Hill, North Carolina: University of North Carolina Press.

—— 1977b. 'The office and the *poblador*: perceptions and manipulations of housing authorities by the Lima urban poor', in *Authoritarianism and Corporatism in Latin America*, ed. J. M. Malloy. Pittsburgh: University of Pittsburgh Press.

—— 1977c. 'Bureaucratic demand making and clientelistic participation in Peru', in *Authoritarianism and Corporatism in Latin America*, ed. J. M. Malloy. Pittsburgh: University of Pittsburgh Press.

—— 1978. 'Metropolitan Lima: urban problem-solving under military rule', in *Metropolitan Latin America*, eds. A. Cornelius & R. V. Kemper. Latin American Urban Research, 6. Beverly Hills, California: Sage.

—— 1979. *Poverty and problem-solving under military rule: the urban poor in Lima, Peru*. Texas: University of Texas Press.

—— 1980. *Poverty and Problem solving under Military Rule: The Urban Poor in Lima, Peru*. Austin: University of Texas Press.

Dietz, H., & Palmer, D. S. 1978. 'Citizen Participation under innovative military Corporatism in Peru', in *Citizen and the State: political participation in Latin America*, ed. J. A. Booth & M. A. Seligson. New York: Holmes and Meier.

Dietz, A. G. H., Koth, M. N., & Sivlo, J. A. 1965. *Housing in Latin America*. Cambridge, Mass.: M.I.T. Press.

Dobkin, M. 1962. 'La cultura de la pobreza y el amor mágico: un síndrome en el selva peruana', *America Indigena*, 29:1.

Dobyns, H. E., & Doughty, P. L. 1976. *Peru: a Cultural History*. New York: Oxford University Press.

Dobyns, H. E., & Vasquez, M. C. 1963. *Migración e Integración en el Perú*. Lima: Ed. Estudios Andinos.

Dollfus, D. 1958. 'Lima: quelques aspects de la capitale de Peru en 1958', *Cahiers d'Outre-Mer*, 11:43.

Dorich, T. L. 1961. 'Urbanization and physical planning in Peru', in *Urbanization in Latin America*, ed. P. M. Hauser. Paris: UNESCO.

Doughty, P. L. 1970. 'Behind the back of the city: "provincial" life in Lima, Peru', in *Peasants in Cities*, ed. W. Mangin. Boston: Houghton Mifflin.

—— 1972. 'Peruvian migrant identity in an urban milieu', in *Anthropology of Urban Environments*, eds. T. Weaver & D. White. Monographs 11. Boulder, Col.: Society for Applied Anthropology.

—— 1974. 'Social policy and urban growth in Lima', in *Peruvian Nationalism: A Corporatist Revolution*, ed. D. Chaplin. New York: Dutton-Transaction.

Durand, J. 1964. 'Castas y clases en el habla de Lima', *Caravelle*, 3.

Dwyer, D. J. 1975. *People and Housing in Third World Cities*. London: Longman.

Figueroa, A. 1974. *Estructura del consumo y distribución de ingreso en Lima Metropolitana 1968–69*. Lima: Pontificia Universidad Católica.

Fitzgerald, E. V. K. 1976. *The State and Economic Development: Peru Since 1968*. Department of Applied Economics, Occasional Paper 49. Cambridge: Cambridge University Press.

—— 1979. *The Political Economy of Peru 1956–78*. Cambridge: Cambridge University Press.

Fried, J. M. 1959. 'Occupation and mental health among Indian migrants in Peru', in *Culture and Mental Health: Cross Cultural Studies*, ed. M. M. Opler. New York: Macmillan.

Fried, J. M., & Gleicher, P. 1961. 'Some sources of residential satisfaction in an urban slum', *American Institute of Planners Journal*, 27:4.

Gianella, J. 1970. *Marginalidad en Lima Metropolitana*. Lima: Cuadernos DESCO A8.

Goldrich, D. 1970. 'Political organization and the politicization of the poblador', *Comparative Political Studies*, 3:2.

Goldrich, D. *et al.* 1967. 'The political integration of lower class settlement in Chile and Peru', *Studies in Comparative International Development*, 3:1. Also in *Masses in Latin America*, ed. I. L. Horowitz. New York: Oxford University Press. 1970.

Grenfell, M., & Robles Rivas, D. 1965. 'Squatters in Peru', *Architects Year Book*, 11.

Guerrero de los Ríos, R., & Sánchez León, A. 1977. *La Trampa Urbana; Ideología problemas urbanos: el caso de Lima*. Praxis 7. Lima: DESCO.

Gurrieri, A. 1969. *La Mujer joven y el trabajo: un estudio en el Perú*. Santiago: Instituto Latino americano de Planficación Económica y Social.

Gutíerrez Vidalon, H. 1969. *Tugurio estudio de casos*. Lima: Plandemet.

Hake, A. 1977. *African Metropolis*. Brighton: Sussex University Press.

Hall, F. M. 1965. 'Family planning in Lima, Peru', 'Birth Control in Lima, Peru', *Milbank Memorial Fund Quarterly*, 43:4.

Hammel, E. A. 1961. 'The family cycle in a Peruvian slum and village', *American Anthropologist*, 63:5.

—— 1964. 'Some characteristics of rural village and urban slum populations of the coast of Peru', *Southwestern Journal of Anthropology*, 20:4.

Hargous, S. 1972. *Les déracinés du Quart Monde*. Paris: Maspero.

Harris, W. D. 1971. *The Growth of Latin American Cities*. Athens, Ohio: Ohio University Press.

Harris, W. D. *et al.* 1963. *Housing in Peru*. Department of Social Affairs. Washington, D.C.: Pan American Union.

Henry, Etienne. 1978. *La Escena Urbana: Estado y Movimientos de Pobladores 1968–76*. Lima: Pontificia Universidad Católica del Perú.

Herbold, C. F. 1971. 'Peru', in *The Urban Development of Latin America 1750–1920*, ed. R. Morse. Center for Latin American Studies. Stanford, California: Stanford University Press.

Isbell, B. J. 1973. 'Andean structures and activities: towards a study of transformations of traditional concepts in a Central highland peasant community', Ph.D. Thesis, University of Illinois.

—— 1974. 'The influence of migrants upon traditional social and political concepts: a Peruvian case study', in *Latin American Urban Research*, 4. eds. W. A. Cornelius & F. M. Trueblood. Beverly Hills, California: Sage.

Jaworski, H. 1969. *Políticas de vivienda popular y barrios marginales*. Lima: Cuadernos DESCO A1.

Jongkind, F. 1974. 'A reappraisal of the role of regional associations in Lima, Peru: an epistemological perspective', *Comparative Studies in Society and History*, 16:4.

Kemper, R. V. 1971. *Bibliografía comentada sobre la antropológica urbana Americana Latina*. Latin America Reprint Series 393. Berkeley, California: Institute of International Studies.

Laite, A. J. 1977. 'The Migrant Worker: A Case Study of Industrialization and Social Stratification in Highland Peru', Ph.D. Thesis, University of Manchester.

Leeds, A. 1969. 'The Significant Variables determining the Character of Squatter Settlements', *America Latina*, 12.

—— 1971. 'The Culture of poverty concept: conceptual, logical and empirical problems with perspectives from Brazil and Peru', in *The Culture of Poverty: a critique*, ed. E. Leacock. New York: Simon and Schuster.

—— 1974. 'Housing settlement types, arrangements for living, proletarianization and the social structure of the city', in *Latin American Urban Research*, 4, eds. W. A. Cornelius & F. M. Trueblood. Beverly Hills, California: Sage.

Leeds, A.& E. 1968. 'Brazil and the myth of urban rurality: urban experience, work and values in the "squatments" of Rio de Janeiro and Lima', in *City and Country in the Third World*, ed. A. J. Field. Cambridge, Mass.: Schenkman.

—— 1976. 'Accounting for behavioural differences: three political systems and the responses of squatters in Brazil, Peru and Chile', in *The City in Comparative Perspective: Cross-National research and new directions in Theory*, eds. J. Walton & L. H. Masotti. Beverly Hills, California: Sage.

Lewis, R. A. 1973. *Employment, Income and the Growth of Barriadas in Lima, Peru*. Latin American Studies Program, Dissertation Series 46. Ithaca, N.Y.: Cornell University Press.

Lloyd, P. C. 1967. *Africa in Social Change*. Harmondsworth: Penguin.

—— 1979. *Slums of Hope?* Harmondsworth: Penguin.

Lindenberg, K. 1969. 'The effect of negative sanctions on politicization among lower class sectors of Santiago, Chile and Lima, Peru', Ph.D. Thesis, University of Oregon.

Lobo, S. B. 1976. 'Urban adaptation among Peruvian migrants', in *New Approaches to the Study of Migration*, eds. D. Guillet & D. Uzzell., Rice University Studies, 62:3. Houston, Texas: Rice University Press.

—— 1977. 'Kin Relationships and the Process of Urbanization in the Squatter Settlements of Lima, Peru', Ph.D. Thesis, Arizona University.

Lomnitz, L. de. 1977. *Networks and Marginality*. London: Academic Press.

Long, N. 1973. 'The role of regional associations in Peru', in *The Process of Urbanization*, eds. M. Drake *et al*. Bletchley: Open University.

Low, S. H. 1975. 'The Social and Spatial Organization of a Peruvian Barriada', Ph.D. Thesis, Harvard University.

Lowder, S. 1970. 'Lima's population growth and the consequences for Peru', in *Urban Population Growth and Migration in Latin America*, eds. B. Roberts and S. Lowder. Centre for Latin American Studies, Monograph Series 2. Liverpool: University of Liverpool Press.

—— 1974. 'Migration and Urbanisation in Peru', in *Spatial Aspects of Development*, ed. B. S. Hoyle. London: Wiley.

Lowenthal, A. F. (ed.) 1975. *The Peruvian Experiment: Continuity and Change under Military Rule*. Princeton, N.J.: Princeton University Press.

Lutz, T. 1969. 'Political Socialization and the developing political subcultures among Squatters in Panama City, Guayaquil and Lima: Comparisons of attitudes in Organized and Unorganized Squatter Settlements', Ph.D. Thesis, Georgetown University.

MacEwen Scott, A. M. 1978. 'Occupational careers and economic strategies of the Working Class of Lima, Peru', in *Development Research Digest 1: Urban Growth and Urban Poverty*, ed. Z. Mars. Brighton: Institute of Development Studies.

McKenney, J. W. 1969. 'Voluntary association and political integration: an exploratory study of the role of voluntary association membership in the political socialisation of urban Lower class residents in Santiago and Lima', Ph.D. Thesis, University of Oregon.

Málaga, A. A. 1962. *Las barriadas y su integración a la vida urbana*. Lima: Instituto de Planeamiento.

Malpica Silva, C. 1968. *Los dueños del Perú*. Lima: Ed. Ensayas Sociales.

Manaster, K. A. 1968. 'The problem of urban squatters in developing countries: Peru', *Wisconsin Law Review*, 23:1.

Mangin, W. 1959. 'The role of regional associations in the adaptation of rural populations in Peru', *Sociologus*, 9:11. Also in *Contemporary Cultures and Societies in Latin America*, eds. R. N. Adams & B. Heath. New York: Random House. 1965.

—— 1960. 'Mental health and migration to cities: a Peruvian case', *Annals of New York Academy of Sciences*, 84. Also in *Urbanization and Change*, eds. P. Meadows & E. Mizruchi. Reading, Mass.: Addison Wesley. 1969.

—— 1966. 'Latin American squatter settlements: a problem and a solution', *Latin American Research Review*, 2:3.

—— 1967. 'Squatter settlements', *Scientific American*, 217:4. Also in *Readings in the Social Sciences*, ed. H. Harlow. San Francisco: Freeman. 1969. And in *Cities, their Origin, Growth and Human Impact*, ed. K. Davis. San Francisco: Freeman. 1973.

—— 1968. 'Poverty and politics in cities of Latin America', in *Power, Poverty and Urban Policy*, eds. W. Bloomberg & H. T. Schmandt. Beverly Hills, California: Sage.

—— 1970a. 'Urbanization case history in Peru', *Architectural Design*, 8. Also in *Peasants in Cities*, ed. W. Mangin. Boston: Houghton Mifflin. 1970.

—— 1970b. 'Tales from the Barriadas', in *Peasants in Cities*, ed. W. Mangin. Boston: Houghton Mifflin.

—— 1970c. 'Similarities and differences between two types of Peruvian communities', in *Peasants in Cities*, ed. W. Mangin. Boston: Houghton Mifflin.

—— 1973. 'Sociological, cultural and political characteristics of some urban migrants in Peru', in *Urban Anthropology*, ed. A. Southall. New York: Oxford University Press.

Mangin, W., & Cohen, J. 1965. 'Cultural and Psychological Characteristics of Mountain Migrants to Lima', *Sociologus*, 14:1.

Mangin, W., & Turner, J. C. 1969. 'Benavides and the barriada movements', in *Shelter and Society*, ed. P. Oliver. New York: Barrie & Rockcliff.

Marret, R. 1969. *Peru*. London: Knight.

Martínez, H. 1969. *Las migraciones internas del Perú*. Caracas: Ed. Monte Ávila.

Matos Mar, J. 1961. 'The barriadas of Lima: an example of integration into Urban Life', in *Urbanization in Latin America*, ed. P. M. Hauser. Paris: UNESCO.

—— 1964. 'El caso del Perú: consideraciones sobre su situación social como marco de referencia al problema de Lima', *America Latina*, 7:1.

—— 1966. *Estudio de las Barriadas Limenas*. Lima: Instituto de Estudios Peruanos.

—— 1968. *Urbanización y Barriadas en America del Sur*. Lima: Instituto de Estudios Peruanos.

Matos Mar, J. *et al.* 1971. *Perú: Hoy*. Mexico City: Siglo Veintiuno.

Mesa-Largo, C. 1978. *Social Security in Latin America*. Pittsburgh: University of Pittsburgh Press.

Michl, S. 1973. 'Urban squatter organization as a national government tool: the case of Lima, Peru', in *Latin American Urban Research*, 3, eds. F. F. Rabinowitz & F. M. Trueblood. Beverly Hills, California: Sage.

Miller, J., & Gakenheimer, R. A. 1971. *Latin American Urban Policies and the Social Sciences.* Beverly Hills, California: Sage.

Millones, L. 1975. *La cultura colonial urbana: una hipótesis del trabajo para el estudio de las poblaciones tugurizadas.* Lima: Cisepa.

—— 1978. *Tugurio: La Cultura de Los Marginados.* Lima: Instituto Nacional de Cultura.

Ministerio del Trabajo. 1967. *Diagnóstico de la Situación de Recursos Humanos, Servicio del empleo y Recursos Humanos: Barriadas de Lima.* Lima: Centro de Investigación por Muestreo.

Montoya, M. 1973. 'Pamplona: un caso de movilización a partir de la base', Doctoral Thesis, University of San Marcos, Lima.

Montoya Ramirez, J. 1962. 'La Ley de Remodelación, Saneamiento y Legislación de Barriadas marginales', Doctoral Thesis, University of San Marcos, Lima.

Montoya Rojas, R. 1967. 'La migración interna en el Perú: un caso concreto', *America Latina*, 10:4.

Myers, S. K. 1973. *Language Shift among migrants to Lima, Peru.* Dept of Geography Research Papers 147. Chicago: University of Chicago Press.

Nieto P., L. 1974. 'Historia y Situación socio-económica del pueblo joven "Medalla Milagrosa"', Bachelor's Thesis, University of San Marcos, Lima.

ONEC (Oficina Nacional de Estadísticas y Censas). 1969. *Informe de la encuesta de fecundidad en el Agustino.* Lima.

—— 1973. 'Los Pueblos Jóvenes en el Perú', *Boletín de Análisis demográfico.* Año 1972, 13. Lima.

Owens, R. J. 1963. *Peru.* London: Oxford University Press.

Palmer, D. S. 1973. *'Revolution from above': Military Government and Popular Participation in Peru, 1968–1972.* Latin American Studies Programme, Dissertation Series 47. Ithaca, N.Y.: Cornell University Press.

Paredes, M. Koth de. 1973. 'Urban Community Organization in Peru', Ph.D. Thesis, M.I.T. Press.

Patch, R. 1961. 'Life in a Callejón: a study of urban disorganisation', *American Universities Field Staff Reports. West Coast South America Series*, 8:6.

—— 1967. 'La Parada, Lima's Market', *American Universities Field Staff Reports, West Coast South American Series*, 14.

Peattie, L. R. 1968. *The View from the 'Barrio'.* Ann Arbor: University of Michigan Press.

Perlman, J. E. 1976. *Myths of Marginality: The Urban Squatter in Brazil.* Berkeley, California: University of California Press.

Petras, J., & Laporte, R. 1971. *Perú: Transformación Revolucionaria o Modernización?* Buenos Aires: Amorrotu.

Phillip, G. D. E. 1978. *The Rise and Fall of the Peruvian Military Radicals. 1968–76.* London: Athlone Press.

Pike, F. B. 1967. *The Modern History of Peru.* New York: Praeger.

Plandemet. 1968. *Estudio de tugurios en los distritos de Jesús María y la Victoria.* Lima: Plan de desarrollo metropolitano Lima–Callao.

Portes, A. 1972. 'Rationality in the slum: an essay on interpretive sociology', *Comparative Studies in Society and History*, 14.

Powell, S. 1969. 'Political participation in the barriadas: a case study', *Comparative Political Studies*, 2.

Pratt, R. B. 1968. 'Organizational participation, politicization and development: a study of political consequences of participation in community association in four lower class urban settlements in Chile and Peru', Ph.D. Thesis, University of Oregon.

Quijano O., A. 1965. 'La emergencia del grupo "cholo" y sus consecuencias en la sociedad peruana', *7° Congreso Latino Americano de Sociología*.

—— 1968. 'Tendencies in Peruvian development and class structure', in *Reform or Revolution*, eds. J. Petras & M. Zeitlin. Greenwich, Conn.: Fawcett.

—— 1972. 'La constitución del "mundo" de la marginalidad urbana', *Revista Latino-Americana de estudios urbanos regionales*, 2:5.

—— 1974. 'The marginal pole of the economy and the marginalised labour force', *Economy and Society*, 3:4.

Riofrio B., G. 1978. *Se Busca Terreno para Próxima Barriada*. Lima: DESCO.

Roberts, B. R. 1973. *Organising Strangers: poor families in Guatemala City*. Texas: University of Texas Press.

—— 1974a. 'Migración Urbana', *Ethnica*, 6.

—— 1974b. 'The Interrelationships of City and provinces in Peru and Guatemala', in *Latin American Urban Research*, 4, eds. W. A. Cornelius & F. M. Trueblood. Beverly Hills, California: Sage.

Robin, J. P., & Terzo, F. C. 1972. *Urbanization in Peru*. International Urbanization Survey. New York: Ford Foundation.

Robles Rivas, D. 1969. *El Proceso de Urbanización y los Sectores Populares en Lima*. Lima: Cuadernos DESCO A1.

—— 1972. *'Development Alternatives for the Peruvian barriadas'*, in *Latin American Urban Research*, 2, eds. G. Geisse & J. E. Hardoy. Beverly Hills, California: Sage.

Rodríguez, A. et al. 1969. *Aportes a la comprensión de un fenómeno urbano: la Barriada*. Lima: Cuadernos DESCO A2.

—— 1973. *Segregación residencial y Desmovilización Política: el caso de Lima*. Buenos Aires: ed. Siap-Planteos.

Rodríguez, A., & Jaworski, H. 1969. *Vivienda en Barriadas*. Lima: Cuadernos DESCO A4.

Rodríguez, A., Riofrio, G., & Welsh, E. 1973. *De Invasores a Invadidos*. Lima: DESCO.

Ross, M. H. 1973. *The Political Integration of Urban Squatters*. Evanston, Illinois: Northwestern University Press.

Rotondo, H. 1961. 'Psychological and mental health problems of urbanization based on case studies in Peru', in *Urbanization in Latin America*, ed. P. M. Hauser. Paris: UNESCO.

Rutte G., A. 1973. *Simplemente Explotadas: el Mundo de las Empleadas Domésticas de Lima*. Lima: DESCO.

Safa, H. I. 1974. *The Urban Poor in Puerto Rico*. New York: Holt Rinehart & Winston.

Sánchez León, A. et al. 1979. *Tugurización en Lima Metropolitana*. Lima: DESCO.

Santos, M. 1975. 'The Periphery at the Pole: Lima, Peru', in *The Social Economy of Cities*, eds. G. Gappert & H. Rose. Urban Affairs Annual Reviews 9. Beverly Hills, California: Sage.

—— 1976. 'Articulation of Modes of Production and the two currents of urban economy – wholesalers of Lima, Peru', *Pacific Viewpoint*, 3.

Sarfati Larson, M., & Eisen Bergman, A. 1969. *Social Stratification in Peru*. Institute of International Studies. Berkeley, California: University of California Press.

Simmons, O. G. 1965. 'The criollo outlook in the mestizo culture of coastal Peru',

Bibliography 155

in *Contemporary Culture and Societies of Latin America*, eds. D. B. Heath & R. N. Adams. New York: Random House.

SINAMOS, 1973. *Diagnóstica Nacional de la Problemática de los Pueblos Jóvenes*. Lima.

Skeldon, R. 1976. 'Regional associations and population migration in Peru: an interpretation', *Urban Anthropology*, 5:3.

—— 1977. 'Regional Associations: a note on opposed interpretations', *Comparative Studies in Society and History*.

Slater, D. 1972. 'Spatial Aspects of the Peruvian Socio-economic System. 1925–1968', Ph.D. Thesis, University of Sussex.

Smith, M. L. 1971. 'Institutionalised Servitude: the female domestic servant in Lima, Peru', Ph.D. Thesis, University of Indiana.

—— 1973. 'Domestic service as a channel of upward mobility for the lower class women: the Lima case', in *Female and Male in Latin America; essays*, ed. A. Pescatello. Pittsburgh: University of Pittsburgh Press.

—— 1975. 'The female domestic servant and social change: Lima, Peru', in *Women Cross-Culturally*, ed. L. R. R. Leavatt. Chicago: Aldine.

Solari, A. E., Franco, R., & Vutkovitz, J. 1976. *Teoría, Acción Social y Desarrollo en América Latina*. Mexico City: Siglo Veintiuno.

Stepan, A. 1978. *The State and Society: Peru in Comparative Perspective*. Princeton, N. J.: Princeton University Press.

Stokes, C. 1972. 'A theory of slums', *Land Economics*, 8:3.

Stycos, J. M. 1965. 'Female employment and fertility in Lima, Peru', *Milbank Memorial Fund Quarterly*, 63:1.

—— 1965. 'Social class and preferred family size in Peru', *American Journal of Sociology*, 22:6.

Tapia Garcia, A. 1971. *Acción de las Instituciones de Crédito especializadas en Financiamiento de Viviendo en el Perú*.

Thorp, R., & Bertram, G. 1978. *Peru 1890–1977: Growth and policy in an Open Economy*. London: Macmillan.

Touraine, A. 1976. *Les Sociétés dépendantes*. Paris: Duclot.

Trigoso, J. 1967. *Nacimiento, Vida y Muerte en la Barriadas*. Lima: Centro de Estudios y Promoción de Desarrollo.

Trujillo, A. S. 1968. *El Gobierno Metropolitano y Limatrópoli*. Lima.

Tullis, F. L. 1970. *Lord and Peasant in Peru*. Cambridge, Mass.: Harvard University Press.

Turner, J. F. C. 1963. 'Lima's Barriadas Today', *Architectural Design*, 33:8.

—— 1965. 'Lima's Barriadas and Corralones: Suburbs or Slums', *Ekistics*, 19:112.

—— 1967. 'Barriers and Channels for housing development in Modernising countries', *Journal of the American Institute of Planners*, 32:3. Also in *Peasants in Cities*, ed. W. Mangin. Boston: Houghton Mifflin. 1970.

—— 1968a. 'Uncontrolled urban settlement: problems and policies', *International Social Development Review*, 1.

—— 1968b. 'Architecture that works', *Architectural Design*, 38. Also in *Ekistics*, 27.

—— 1969. *Nueva visión del déficit de vivienda*. Lima: Cuadernos DESCO A1.

Uchoya Reyes, H. E. 1971. *Normas legales de Pueblos Jóvenes*. Lima: Ed. Hew.

Uzzell, J. D. 1972. 'Bound for places I'm not known to: adaptation of migrant and residence in four irregular settlements in Lima, Peru', Ph.D. Thesis, University of Texas.

—— 1974a. 'A strategic analysis of social structure in Lima, using the concept of "plays"', *Urban Anthropology*, 3:1.

—— 1974b. 'Cholos and bureaus in Lima: case history and analysis', *International Journal of Comparative Sociology*, 15.

—— 1974c. 'The interaction of population and locality in the development of squatter settlements in Lima', in *Latin American Urban Research*, 4, eds. W. A. Cornelius & F. M. Trueblood. Beverly Hills, California: Sage.

—— 1976. *From Play lexicons to Disengagement spheres in Peru's Urbanization*. Program of Development Studies, Papers 72. Texas: Rice University Press.

Valdivia Ponce, O. 1970. *Migración Interna a la Metrópoli*. Lima: University of San Marcos.

Vandendries, R. 1973. 'Internal migration and economic development in Peru', in *Latin American Modernization Problems*, ed. R. E. Scott. Urbana, Illinois: University of Illinois Press.

Vasquez, M., & Dobyns, H. 1963. *Migración e Integración*. Lima: Instituto de Estudios Andinos.

Walter, J. P. 1975. *Deprived urban youth: an economic and cross cultural analysis of the United States, Colombia and Peru*. New York: Praeger.

Watson, J. L. (ed.) 1977. *Between Two Cultures: Migrants and Minorities in Britain*. Oxford: Basil Blackwell.

Webb, R. C. 1977. *Government Policy and the Distribution of income in Peru 1963–1973*. Cambridge, Mass.: Harvard University Press.

Weisslitz, J. 1973. 'Migración rural e integración urbana en el Perú', in *Imperialismo y Urbanización en America Latina*, ed. M. Castells. Barcelona: Ed. Gustavo Gili.

Weller, R. H. 1974. 'The structural assimilation of in-migrants to Lima, Peru', *International Migration Review*, 8:4.

Welsh, E. 1970. *Bibliografía sobre el crecimiento dinámico de Lima, referente al proceso de urbanización en el Perú*. Lima: Cuadernos DESCO A5.

Wils, F. 1975. *Industrialists, Industrialisation and the Nation-state in Peru*. The Hague: Institute of Social Research.

Woy, S. A. 1978. 'Infrastructure of participation in Peru: SINAMOS', in *Citizen and State: Political Participation in Latin America*, 1, eds. J. A. Booth & M. A. Seligson. New York: Holmes and Meier.

Index

African cities, 4–5
Aguirre Gamio, Hernando, 36
Alderson-Smith, Gavin, 8, 39
Altimirano, T., 8
Andrews, F. M., 95
AP (Acción Popular), 44
APRA (Alianza Popular
  Revolucionaria Americana), 22,
  43, 45
Aragón, Sr, 113–14
Arequipa, 1, 3–4, 26, 29–30
Asociación de Pobladores, 45,
  58–60, 82ff., 94ff., 102ff.

Bambarén, Bishop Luis, 45
barriadas, 4, 12, 30; characteristics
  of, 10, 14, 144; diversity of, 14,
  47–8, 50–2, 90, 140–2; evictions
  from, 57–8, 64, 88, 93; growth of,
  3, 5–6, 35–6, 40–1, 47, 115, 140,
  142–3; housing in, 42, 47–50,
  55–6, 63–4, 140, 142; invasions of,
  3–5, 35, 40–1, 43–5, 57, 130, 140,
  142–3; land titles in, 6, 42, 44–6,
  50, 91, 97, 100, 106, 112;
  remodelling of, 44–5, 47, 97–8,
  100, 103, 108; services in, 6, 45,
  48–9, 54, 56, 59, 88, 91–100, 105,
  107–8, 112, 141; see also land
Belaúnde Terry, Fernando, 22, 44–5,
  54, 58–9, 128
Beltrán, Pedro, 37, 43
building societies, 36–7, 43, 143

Callao, 1, 2, 9, 25, 33–5, 37, 39, 54,
  69, 90, 100, 104, 117, 120
callejones, 3, 39, 40, 130
Cardoso, F. H., 116–17
children, 29, 49, 56–7, 62, 70–1,
  76–7, 117, 120, 145; psychological
  disorders of, 78, 83–4, 111, 120
cholo, 11–12, 21, 34, 115–16, 118
class, 23, 128, 131–2; categories, 13,
  124–5, 136–7, 140
157

class-consciousness, 134–6
Club de Madres, 55, 59, 84–5, 87,
  90, 95–6, 99, 103, 111, 119
clubs, village, 4, 7–8, 10, 62, 79–81,
  85, 89, 120–1, 142; see also
  Huancaray club
collective action, 7, 14, 89–92, 130,
  133–4, 140, 142
Collier, D., 40–2, 46
community, 9–10, 87, 89, 91;
  activity, 85, 88ff., 111, 113;
  conflict, 111–12; contributions, 7,
  60, 82–3, 85, 88, 98, 107–9, 113;
  labour, 7, 64, 92, 96–7, 107, 128;
  organizations, 141–4; solidarity,
  110–11, 113, 134, 140
Cornelius, W., 101
corralón, 3, 39–40, 42, 52, 62, 83,
  88–9, 93, 110, 115–16, 128, 140
Cotler, J., 34, 41
creoles, 19
crime, 88, 96, 122
criollos, 11, 21, 90
Cuzco, 1, 3–4, 17–19, 20, 26, 29–30,
  61, 68

Deler, J. P., 33, 34, 38, 40
Delgado, C., 45, 48
DESCO (Centro de Estudios y
  Promoción de Desarrollo), 34, 37,
  45, 48–50
Dietz, H. A., 93
Dobyns, H. E., 1
Doughty, P. L., 1, 7
dualist development theories, 118–19
Dwyer, D. J., 37

education, 6, 27, 50, 52, 55, 59, 61,
  65, 72, 76, 83, 87, 111, 120, 128,
  132; secondary, 27, 65, 71, 84;
  tertiary, 71; parents' aspirations
  for, 71–2, 76, 109, 120
Eisen Bergman, A., 24–6, 34
employment, 50–1, 68–74, 123–6,

160   *Index*

Velasco Alvarado, Juan, 22, 45, 121,
128

Watson, J. L., 8

Webb, R. C., 28, 125–8
women: education of, 65, 70, 84;
employment of, 62, 69–70, 73, 84;
social status of, 95–6